19

THIS BOOK SHOULD BE RETURNED ON OR BEFORE THE LATEST
DATE SHOWN TO THE LIBRARY FROM WHICH IT WAS BORROWED

CHORLEY

Cuc to SCg
3/04

2 JAN 2008

17 JAN 2002

4 JUL 2002

18. JAN 08

11. MAR 06

15 NOV 2006

17 OCT 2008

ARLINGTON

24. MAR 03

15. NOV 06.

9 JUN 2009

ECCLESTON
5/03

26. OCT 07

AUTHOR	CLASS
SUTCLIFFE, P.	780.422 SUT

TITLE
The Beatles shadow

the beatles' shadow

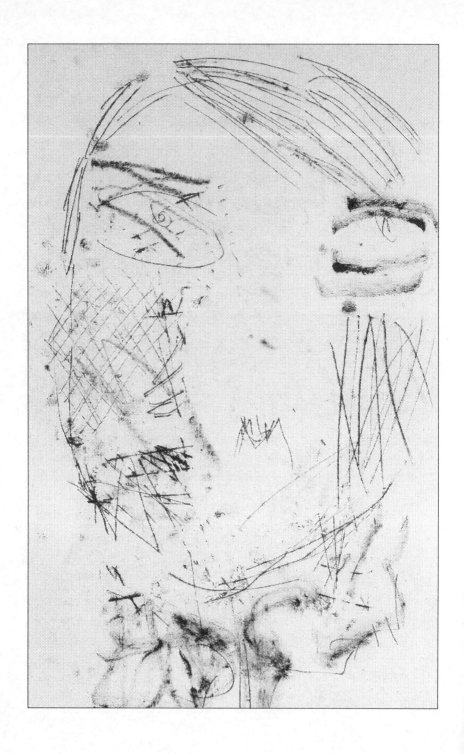

the beatles' shadow

STUART SUTCLIFFE

& his lonely hearts club

PAULINE SUTCLIFFE

WITH DOUGLAS THOMPSON

SIDGWICK & JACKSON

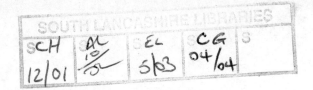
08604319

First Published 2001 by Sidgwick & Jackson
an imprint of Pan Macmillan Ltd
Pan Macmillan, 20 New Wharf Road, London N1 9RR
Basingstoke and Oxford
Associated companies throughout the world
www.panmacmillan.com

ISBN 0 283 07342 X

1 3 5 7 9 8 6 4 2

A CIP catalogue record for this book is available from
the British Library.

Typeset by SX Composing DTP, Rayleigh, Essex
Printed and bound in Great Britain by
Mackays of Chatham plc, Chatham, Kent

For my family

Acknowledgements

With a little help from your friends . . . A generous thank you to Gordon Wise for his brilliant inspiration of introducing me to Douglas Thompson who, with his sensitivity, good humour and experience, has helped me honour my brother's life and art with this book. Also, much gratitude to Ingrid Connell for her focus and skills.

'John liked and wanted strong personalities, and
I think what he learned from Stuart was a certain mystic quality.
Stuart was different and that attracted John.'

Bill Harry

'We have improved a thousandfold since our arrival
and Allan Williams who is here at the moment says there
is no group in Liverpool to touch us.'

Stuart Sutcliffe reporting from Hamburg on the success
of the Beatles in a letter to his sister Pauline

'They are not ever jealous for the cause,
But jealous for they are jealous.'

Shakespeare, *Othello*

Contents

List of Art Works

Unless otherwise stated, all artworks are from the Pauline Sutcliffe collection.

prologue

Magical History Tour

'Life without memory is no life at all.'

Luis Buñuel

HAPPILY, I SHARE my birth day with Elvis Presley. I first found that out from my older brother, Stuart. He loved Elvis. Stuart wanted more than most. He loved life. He locked on to the Elvis energy, yet it was never about teenage rebellion but, rather, wanting to run at the horizon and leap as fast and as enjoyably as possible over it. Everything that increased his pulse rate and his curiosity was special. His mind was always racing, intrigued by people, music, and art, and all the shades and aspects of life and imagination that gave so much purpose, a resonance, to his own. Our parents, especially my mother, set the rules of the race for all of us. For Stuart, it was a sprint. He died on 10 April 1962, aged twenty-one. He died abroad, and such were the complex rules of returning him home for a family funeral I never saw him in death: he was locked in his coffin. The German undertakers said his hair was combed forward and he looked like one of the Beatles, which was perceptive of them. He was.

Stuart Sutcliffe was an original Beatle, John Lennon's intimate friend, one of the young Liverpool boys who were there as a musical legend was being created; but also being conjured up were events, some that can only be thought of as happenstance, others severely premeditated, that brought my family and the Beatles into lifelong association. There have been few benefits for me other than friendships like that with Cynthia Lennon. Overwhelmingly, there has been a sadness and suffering that began not all that long after my brother christened himself and his young friends the Beatles.

My family have lived with none of the benefits but all of the enmities and rivalries, and sometimes the horrors, of our founding association with the most popular musical group of all time. As it turned out, the Beatles so easily could have been Stuart Sutcliffe's Lonely Hearts' Club Band, for Stuart, who played in and named the group, became (like Sergeant Pepper) a ghostly, fantasy figure, just a shadow, in the greatest show business story ever. Depending on your arithmetic he was the fourth or the fifth Beatle but after he died he was lost, the forgotten Beatle. Especially to the Beatles. They circled the wagons. They were ordinary young men caught up in extraordinary and fast-changing times, and by the mid-1960s they were the most famous people in the English-speaking world – already mythical to everyone but themselves, trapped as they always would be simply by being Beatles.

Of course, it is a strange world; people *are* particular and peculiar. I do know. I have spent my working life as a social service manager, and as a trained psychotherapist I have confronted and dealt with the elaborate problems that face so many people on a daily basis; often we have high-sounding, technical names for the myriad disorders that can trip up people's lives and those around them.

Since the late 1960s when I was doing my training, generously being given many educational opportunities to learn from some of the very best, I have thought about the real relationship between Stuart and John Lennon. As you become older there is more sense to your world, to your past. I was a teenager when I first met John with Stuart and the glances between them registered but without meaning. I knew there was more to it but it was only later that I had the knowledge to understand. It was a jigsaw puzzle in my mind over the years and probably I did not want to publicly acknowledge the total truth of what they had together. I never saw any shame in any of it but I was reticent. I have kept to myself all

I know and feel about my brother and John for many years. Secrets can be painful. Yet, recent publications have not been as shy as I was. These twenty-first century accounts have lanced the boil for me, made me feel free to tell Stuart and John's real story for the first time. Also, I strongly believe there is a purpose now to be spelling it out for it explains so much about John Lennon and the story of the Beatles. With this book I am completing the foundation of their story, putting the last brick in place. As they say in my business, establishing closure.

I found myself analysing my own thoughts on a comfortable couch on Continental Airlines Flight 57 to America from Gatwick Airport in London. We had just climbed out of the clouds and they had switched off the seat-belt sign and announced a turbulence-free journey to Cleveland, Ohio, the home of the Rock and Roll Hall of Fame and Museum. A glass of long-oaked Chardonnay and some mineral water was presented to me as I looked out at the blue skies; life, if not altogether bump-free, does seem calmer. There was a hopeful horizon for me and I raised the glass in a silent toast. It was to Stuart, to my sister, in memory of my parents and, also, to John Lennon. I included all the others who did not survive long enough alongside that still ongoing phenomenon, the Beatles, in which my brother had such an inspirational and important role. They did not have a choice, but I did. Strangely, as a twenty-first-century Beatlemania manifested itself – worldwide hits, lost tracks rediscovered, Paul McCartney planning a Beatles film – *I* wanted the Beatles out of my life, for ever.

First, there was something I had to achieve and for a long time it had appeared impossible: I needed, metaphorically, to get my brother back, to resurrect him, and in so doing be able, after more than four decades, to lovingly, properly, say farewell to him. And that is what concerned my journey to Cleveland; it revolved around the circle of life whereby, simply, we have to confront and deal with our problems in order to put them to rest. When my brother died the Beatles were an aspiring and popular group in the clubs of

Hamburg. Stuart was pursuing his fabulously promising artistic career, but as often as possible would go to watch and listen to John, George Harrison, Paul McCartney, and the then drummer Pete Best, in the often wild but always exciting clubs of that loose-minded German city. Sometimes he would take up his old position onstage with them. He understood this bunch of boys who played toe-tapping music and enjoyed good times together. There was a Musketeer element about them: they were all teenagers from Liverpool, all, in their own ways, Jack-the-Lads, cheeky, quick-witted, friendly, engaging; on the flip side was the Iago factor: they had all of the individual jealousies brought on, in Stuart's day, by their fledgling success and envy of each other. In later life, I have always had to deal with the dark side.

The Rock and Roll Hall of Fame prompted my decision to escape from it all. I had spent many years collating Stuart's work, more than 250 paintings, works on paper, drawings and sketches, all the memorabilia from the trivia of fame to documents and emotionally revealing letters, into an historic Beatles archive. My mother was fastidious in keeping everything associated with Stuart. He is now accepted in the official art world as a genuine talent; he is certainly highly collectible, and has been exhibited from Liverpool via Japan to Canada and the USA. I was retiring, if that is the correct word in the circumstances, as the executrix and owner of the Stuart Sutcliffe Estate and auctioning the collection, hopefully to an institution that would preserve it and keep Stuart's memory alive. I would feel then that I had done my bit and would be able to free myself from the Beatles. I have been trapped by them most of my life – I wanted to say goodbye. It's been a long goodbye. It will probably only be farewell because you can't blank it all out just by walking away. But the day-to-day hassles, the lawyers, and the phone calls will be gone. That would be an incredible release in itself and might exorcise the ghosts that have haunted me and my family. I have never been in a position to tell the full story before. My mother, always strong and protective and thinking ahead, made my sister Joyce and me swear not to reveal anything we knew, including letters and notes, about the early relationships of the founding Beatles until fifteen years after her death. My mother died in 1983 so since 1998 I have been considering how best to deal with the legacy she left.

The collection, 'Stuart Sutcliffe: From the Beatles to Backbeat', went on display in May 2001, and when it did it ran alongside another fascinating example of Beatles memorabilia. Yoko Ono, who was flown from New York to Cleveland in one of *Rolling Stone* magazine founder Jann Wenner's private jets, spent three hours in town opening the exhibition entitled 'Lennon: His Life and Work'. It seemed so appropriate that Stuart and John should be together in the Rock and Roll Hall of Fame and that their exhibitions would end almost simultaneously in the autumn of 2001. I feel that is how it should have been: Stuart and John reunited after untimely deaths. Their close friendship, their bond, is an essential untold story of the birth of the Beatles. Before Lennon and McCartney, it was Lennon and Sutcliffe, an intense partnership, a jubilant association. Stuart was John's mentor and he tutored John's thinking, which meant he influenced all of his life; Stuart gave John not just knowledge but instilled him with the need to know, to think, and to reflect. John trusted Stuart to tell him the truth. John in return gave Stuart confirmation of his worth. He gave him his utter loyalty and intimacy. They had shared aspirations and dreams. That was their absolute bond.

In turn, I am now close to Cynthia Lennon. I was staying with her in France when she and friends told me of a property that was up for sale. I immediately fell in love with the house, and as a neighbour now see Cynthia even more often. We regularly have dinner together. We are linked by our Beatles association and the early deaths of Stuart and John. One recent evening we were talking over glasses of wine and Cynthia said to me, 'I think it's time to put our boys to bed.' I said, 'I can't yet – I've just got mine back.' We locked eyes for a moment and Cynthia understood: I had to give Stuart his place in the world so that I could move on. I am going to change many perceptions the world has of the Beatles. I have waited many years but now it is my turn. Jetting to the Rock and Roll Hall of Fame, it all seemed incredible. It also feels like yesterday. All the reminiscences are reeled, like film, in my mind; a flick of a mental switch and I see it all: I know it will add to our understanding of the of the Beatles phenomenon that I witnessed at its very beginning.

one

Family Affairs

'I looked up to Stu, I depended on him to tell me the truth.
Stu would tell me if something was good and I'd believe him.'

John Lennon

I WAS A NAÏVE, tiny thing, but I knew instinctively when I walked into that dingy hall in May 1960 that something tremendous was happening. Or about to. I don't know if it was me or the occasion, but the atmosphere was palpable. It was like going to a Grand Prix race, where it can all end in either a car crash or a hero splashed in champagne and euphoria. I was only fifteen years old, but I sensed that what was going on would transmute the scruffy surroundings. And it was one of the most thrilling moments of my young life the first time I saw Stuart with John, Paul, George, and Tommy Moore, who was the drummer before Pete Best; this was the paradigm Beatles. John, just eighteen, Paul, seventeen, and sixteen-year-old George had performed as Johnny and the Moondogs, the act that developed from John's original group, the Quarrymen; when Stuart joined he named them the Beetles. They became the Beatals which, after modifications – the Silver Beetles, the Silver Beatles – will live on, as far as I can know, for ever. My first sight of them that early summer was as the Silver Beatles. I felt my nerves were plugged into the electricity socket.

Up on stage Stuart, just a few months older than John, and the others looked much more mature than they were. They wore black shirts, tight black jeans, and two-tone shoes, their uniform. They also appeared to know what they were doing. They strutted about and played with wires – George had graduated from being an

11

apprentice electrician at Blackler's department store – and even the microphone tied with grubby garden string to a broom handle didn't detract from what I saw as the glamour of the moment. Stuart was moving an amplifier and John was fooling around with a guitar. Paul and George were strumming away but looking very serious. I don't even remember the name of the place but on other nights this seedy joint was a strip club and, given the age of the 'girls', maybe that was the reason for the bad lighting.

These boys all looked pale under the spotlight – a glaring light bulb that kept flickering until George went over and fiddled with it. They were not yet familiar with the art, or the need, for stage make-up. It was how Hollywood portrayed decadent Paris jazz clubs, but this poorly lighted backstreet venue, complete with defaulting sound systems and sparking, smoking electric wires, was more Ken Dodd slapstick than Miles Davis riffs. I thought it was the London Palladium. My brother had made it. He was no longer at home in front of the mirror mimicking a rock star, curling his lip and doing a hip shake with Elvis spinning on his Dansette turntable; he was up there, onstage. With that Johnny Lennon as the lead singer. My school-playground status was assured. Stuart was no expert musician. He was there for love of John and vice versa. But he was up there being a rock star – and that's what nearly every kid in Liverpool dreamed about being. It was the instant step, the lottery win, to fame and fortune. There were rainbows all over Merseyside but few pots of gold. The Silver Beatles belted out 'All Shook Up' and I thought it was such a triumph. My brother knew all the words. He could sing a whole song. What a star. They all were, but I never had any comprehension then that more than forty years later, alive and dead and in their own ways, they would all remain names to conjure with. I have to shake my head when I think about it for it all seems not so long ago; they were fresh and vibrant, full of energy and alive. So alive and rushing at the world. They caroused on stage, dipping down to play their guitars and hold them towards the audience;

they seemed to be daring us not to have a good time, for they most certainly were.

I screamed my head off with the rest of the girls. At first it seemed the thing to do, and then it was all so natural; it was give and take. The louder we were, the wilder these special Beatles, especially John. He seemed to move faster with every squeal. Stuart was solid and cool, almost disassociated from the enterprise and probably more concerned about trying to work out the chords on his guitar. I didn't have any fears now. Rock and roll clubs were such a new thing that concerts did attract gangs of guys who just wanted to make trouble; the regular complaint was that the girls were paying more attention to the groups than to their Teddy boy friends, and often police vans would park close by as a deterrent. I didn't care about that, and most of the time I forgot I was there as a spy – for my mother. She had encouraged Stuart to take me along and, reluctantly, he did. He was always concerned about me and would all but carry me into dance halls and sit me down on a bum-numbing radiator close to the stage. I'm not tall, and that way he could keep his eye on me. Part of his act was to turn his back to the audience – probably as much to hide his lack of expertise on the bass guitar as a gesture of 'cool'. Once I left my perch when I was asked to dance by a great hulk of a Teddy boy. He was funny and harmless, no chains or knuckleduster rings, but when Stuart turned round and I was not in his vision line he panicked. The next thing he saw was the Ted saying a cheerful thank you and placing me right back up on the radiator. I waved at Stuart and he relaxed. They were truly innocent times for me. Stuart would take me home after the shows and then he would go out with John and the others. I was too young – and a kid sister – to be witness to their teenage goings-on. But I could watch the shows and reported back to my mother the secret that not only were they popular but they were able to play and sing a song from start to finish; for all the family this seemed a rather impressive achievement. And it seemed to give my mother Millie some solace. She was wary of Stuart's association with John, who she also found fascinating and attractive. Yet her overwhelming feeling was fear. She felt something wrong, an intuition, that would always be impenetrable for her, for all of our family; my mother was clever and aware enough to have seen change, but this was chilling prescience. Where did it come from? What was her fear of Stuart becoming a rock and roller?

Everyone always wanted the best for Stuart. He had a talent and a personality that people wanted to nurture. My mother was usurped in the affection of her own family by the arrival of an adopted son. Stuart as *her* first-born and a son could never be replaced. By any of us. He was her passion and so became the whole family's.

None of us wanted it any other way. It was a clannish thing, part of our tartan roots that began with our father, Charles Fergusson Sutcliffe, who was the youngest of four children. Our grandparents were Joseph and Mary Sutcliffe, a Yorkshire-born army major and his Scottish wife. Father was born in Scotland in 1905 and was raised as a High Anglican, went to Hamilton Academy and on to the Civil Service. He had a rebel streak and was given to high spirits after bottles were uncorked. But he reined himself into convention, and as an executive Freemason's son became a civil servant. He'd been a King's Scout, raised a Tory, and enjoyed getting the best sounds possible from the church organ.

The soap-opera part of father's life began early. He married the local butcher's daughter. This is not how his parents had predicted marital events, but there were clearly happy moments for they had three sons and a daughter from their ten-year marriage. My mother, Martha Cronin, was born in Lanarkshire in 1907, the last of nine daughters of a retired steel-industry executive, Matthew Cronin, and his wife, Agnes. Matthew Cronin, vaguely related to the writer A.J. Cronin, had Irish roots but was raised in America before settling in Scotland. My mother was the last straw in their desperation for a male heir. Just six months after my mother was born this set of grandparents adopted a boy, a longed-for son.

The boy became the focus of their lives and my mother never had their total love. She talked to me with a terrible sadness about how remote and austere her parents had always seemed, especially her mother. Which is why she gave all of us all her love but Stuart, being the first-born, got the full impact. With hindsight, the foundations for even greater hurt were laid then.

The Cronins were Roman Catholics; their church in the village of Wishaw had been built with funds raised by Matthew and other wealthy Catholics. My mother experienced religious prejudice. She said that, when she was growing up, to be a Catholic was like being a leper. An outcast. When she walked with her family to church – the one they had helped build – abuse was screamed at them. Sometimes stones were thrown at them. My mother went to a convent school and was taught by Franciscan nuns; she was going to be a Catholic missionary, and at eighteen she joined a Franciscan religious order in Yorkshire to prepare for work as a teacher in Africa. It was an open order, and her training included two years' study at the College of Ripon and York St John. She was too delicate for the convent and left, always I think disappointed, before her final vows. She went back to Scotland in pitiful health, malnourished and with abscesses on her spine. She had to be cared for for six months before she began teacher training.

When my parents met it was a magic moment because, for all the tragedy that would befall them, they always loved each other, often through difficult husband-and-wife times. My mother was instantly taken with father who was artistic, musical and worldly. He was also married.

But he seemed so different from any man my mother had met before. They were an odd couple. He was tall, she was tiny, but they matched. Yet my father had to free himself from his marriage to another Martha. The names were easy to resolve: mother became Millie forever more. The legalities were not so simple.

My parents' affair was appalling, for in father's strait-laced family environment a miserable marriage was acceptable, the shame of divorce was not. My father did divorce. The Cronins were perhaps more broad-minded but as Roman Catholics would not condone a marriage between their daughter and a Protestant divorcee. Father lost his Civil Service job and my parents their families who disowned them. They married in a civil ceremony and moved to England, where my father tried different work in London and Manchester. They returned to Scotland for Stuart's birth, settled in Edinburgh, and my father became a marine engineer with the John Brown shipyard in Glasgow. *Our* family was started.

Home for the first three years of Stuart's life was a tall house in an elegant, sophisticated terraced row in Edinburgh's Chalmers Street. Joyce was born there in March 1942. A year later father was drafted as an essential war worker to the Cammell Laird shipyard in Birkenhead. Merseyside and popular history awaited. They moved to a council-owned bungalow at 17 Sedbergh Drive in Huyton, then just beyond the Liverpool city limits. I was born there on 8 January 1944. My mother used to joke that it must be something in the English water, for within three years of arriving on Merseyside her gall bladder had to be removed, she miscarried twins, and subsequently suffered a severe chest infection which left her with chronic bronchial asthma. It never stopped her smoking. She always wanted to return to Scotland. Her views of the Merseyside environment are not printable. But she had her work ethic and her God-fearing values instilled by the Franciscan nuns who she admired and loved to her dying day. And, I believe, beyond.

She left us at a nursery school and taught children displaced and orphaned by the heavy bombing of the city at a temporary school. The Merseyside area had been the Luftwaffe's prime target outside London, and in a single week in May 1941 more than 150,000 houses had been damaged, 800 people killed and around 50,000 made homeless. It was perilous, and mother crossed Liverpool every day by tram to get to the school, which was in a hospital outbuilding. After the war, and throughout our schooldays, she continued to work full-time as a teacher, mostly in Roman Catholic schools and often in slum areas. Her asthma was severe and she always had to have an inhaler and special tablets with her. In her handbag with her cigarettes. She would be half-dead when she arrived home. But she kept going. She never wanted to be in the kitchen. That was boring – there was action outside it. She was an enthusiastic member of the Labour Party and recorded the Huyton district constituency meeting minutes, working with Harold Wilson who remained in touch with her in his days as Prime Minister. And recommended that the Beatles were awarded their MBEs.

My mother used to canvas for Wilson and also write and deliver his election-address envelopes. Of course, we kids were the postal service. We used to joke about growing up with short fingers from having them trapped in letter boxes so often. But we loved it. We loved her political passion, her social conscience. She was an old-fashioned socialist, a Fabian. We had political gatherings at home before the formal constituency meetings. As a youngster I could tell the distinctions between a Bevanite and a Gaitskellite as easily as the distinction between an Elvis or a Cliff Richard fan.

My mother was always for practical help. If there was a needy child at school who hadn't got a jumper she would give them one of ours. I used to feel guilty that we had so much, but we weren't well off as a family ourselves. The spirit was to be giving, and I don't think she often thought of the consequences – or that she might actually be imposing something on the child in need. She was asked to be a Justice of the Peace but she refused on the grounds that one day one of us might come up in court. There was a message in that for us. We were all well aware of what was acceptable behaviour and what wasn't. Stealing would certainly have been regarded as unacceptable, but 'helping yourself' was not stealing. Before Christmas mother would hide boxes of sweets in various places, but we'd find them and take sweets out of the bottom layer before closing them up again. And when our father left his small change on the bedside table, we'd help ourselves. We didn't regard that as stealing. Scrumping – stealing fruit from trees – was OK because the spoils were provided by Nature. One day Joyce and I were surprised to see Stuart working in the bank manager's garden: Stuart was caught stealing apples from his trees, and that was the punishment. Stuart would rather dig the bank manager's garden and keep his crime quiet than face our mother, which tells you an enormous amount about her.

Essentially, she became a single parent when the war ended and father joined the Merchant Navy. From then, her mood swings between strictness and permissiveness were part of taking on solo responsibility. When my father was at home it was happiness time. They had mutual passions, open minds. They liked to argue about everything, especially politics, and enjoyed it. It was a clash of lively intellects. My father would go to church with my mother and supported her political crusades. He prided himself on her need to do her own thing; he was a modern man, a couple of decades before it became fashionable if not always natural.

We grew up surrounded by books, paintings and music. My parents had studied piano as small children and were always playing, and my father did his turn in a dance band and at the cinema for the silent movies. He would play Beethoven and Chopin for us. My mother's forte was the shorter classics, Mozart minuets and 'Träumerei' from Schumann's Kinderscenen. This was before television took over, and we were all expected to do a turn for family entertainment. With Stuart and Joyce, I joined in for 'Little Tommy Tucker' and 'Polly Put the Kettle On'. Polly was my nickname within the family and that song was a cue for teatime. And, being the youngest, Polly did have to put the kettle on.

Stuart's full-time schooling began at Park View Primary School, about half a mile from home. Physically, Stuart resembled my mother – small and slender and short-sighted. From the start, my mother worried about his health. Stuart was examined by a specialist who assured her that Stuart's physical development was perfectly normal. The only childhood illness he had was measles – and we all had it at the same time. My mother was ecstatic: what considerate children we were, little socialists with our collective illness bargain, causing the minimum upheaval in her working life. We were amazingly healthy physically – and apparently psychologically too. Her health was more of a worry. She knew how to handle her asthma attacks but they could happen at any time and were alarming. We learned to cope around the house. One of us would be preparing a cup of tea for her return. We had rotas for our household tasks according to age. I might lay the table for dinner while the older two shopped or cooked, using our father's recipes.

Although housework was an aversion to my mother she was fanatical about cleanliness and tidiness. If it was your turn to dust, you knew you had to lift up the lamps and ornaments and not sweep anything under the carpet. She checked. She was compulsive in her way too: every item had to be back in its exact place. We would rebel but she always won the argument – which gives some idea of how big and powerful she was in our eyes, this tiny, vulnerable woman who could be organizing us like a small regiment one minute and gasping for breath the next.

Our parents were older than most and from a different culture. When my mother went on about 'returning home' we would say, 'This is home.' The unspoken message was, we won't be staying in this country long, so don't get too used to it. As a Scottish Catholic, my mother had her own ideas as to the true capital city of the United Kingdom and succession to the throne. I remember telling my teacher at school that she was wrong, because my mum was a teacher and she *knew*. On special occasions we wore dress kilts and tweed hacking jackets. The kilts were made by my father. We had to kneel to be measured for them – the correct length is from waist to floor when you're kneeling. Joyce had the family tartan, which was Anderson through our father's mother, but we could choose whichever one we liked best. They were beautifully made, with a heavy satin lining down to where the pleats opened. We ate oatcakes and griddle scones, and our breakfast was proper porridge. New Year's Eve, Hogmanay, was the important night in the calendar.

My sister, brother, and I were raised as Anglicans. Mother had left the Roman Catholic Church when she married and spent nine troubled years attending church without taking Holy Communion until she found a priest who would hear her confession. That got her back: on Sunday mornings she would go off to early Mass while we attended a later service at St Gabriel's. Stuart was in the choir from the age of nine until his voice broke. He sang regularly at three services on Sundays and frequently at weddings.

In 1950 we moved to 43 St Anne's Road in Huyton, and a year later Stuart went to school about a four-mile bus ride from us. Ken Horton, who was born on the same day as Stuart, went through Prescot Grammar School with him. Ken was fond of my brother: 'Stuart seemed a little older in the head than most people in the school, more intellectual and better read. He had dead straight, wiry hair which he used to plaster down with a bar of soap in the cloakroom. Being small and wearing big glasses, he did tend to project a swotty image; but he wasn't a swot or at all snooty. He was very bright and intense and studious, especially where art was concerned. The art teacher at Prescot was a large Welshman named Walters, who recognized Stuart's talent for drawing and gave him considerable encouragement. Willy Walters looked a bit like a boxer. He was very gentle and sympathetic, but he wouldn't stand for any messing about in the art room . . . One time we did Matthew Arnold's poem 'The Scholar-Gipsy' in the literature class and afterwards Stuart did a smashing Impressionist-style painting based on it. The rest of us were doing basic stuff like representations of washing-day, but this was 'Art'. Ken said Stuart's early influences were the Impressionists and Van Gogh. I remember him being absorbed with the Pre-Raphaelite painters.

Stuart also got on with his music master who I thought was a bit mad, because he used to dash around in a vast cloak. Joe Kirk was a flamboyant figure, friendly and encouraging – probably quite radical for that time. Stuart, Joyce, and I had taken piano lessons and each of us had a progress book. Stuart's was the only one decorated by gold stars and glowing written reports. We all had fun together – we really did get on as kids. In between lessons we performed our masterwork, 'Music for Percushion'. This involved removing the front of the piano, placing a cushion on the keyboard, sitting on it and bouncing up and down while harpist Stuart plucked at the exposed piano wires: Stuart would abandon his harp and, to a 'percushion' accompaniment, leap from the top of an armchair. Mother, as you might have guessed, did not attend these performances. This was child's play and great fun for us. When Father came home – wait till your father gets home, indeed – he sat with Stuart at the piano and went through what he had learned, which was not a lot. Father was so upset he cancelled the lessons for all of us – without even checking on how well Joyce and I could play.

It was an unusual reaction from my father but he was under much domestic pressure. Something serious was troubling his relationship with my mother – her resentment of my father's first family. She had a fear that he would return to them one day. We children were not even meant to know we had half-brothers and sisters but we did. I witnessed a huge bust-up between my parents about some photographs mother found of my Father visiting his oldest son and family in Australia on one of his long sea trips. It was not long after this that my mother left home. She went to Scotland and took a teaching job. It was the biggest crisis in their marriage.

My father stayed and looked after us. He told us Mother had gone to Scotland to find out if she really wanted to go back for good. I used to go to the post office with Father when he sent her money orders. Thankfully, my mother hated where she was staying and didn't much like the school she was teaching at either. She had agreed to a term's trial and when that ended she came home to us.

But the break solved their problem; she, as we would say now, had needed some space. She also got some new rooms, for in 1953 we moved to 22 Sandiway in Huyton.

Stuart joined the Air Training Corps (ATC) in Huyton village but he was never a spit-and-polish military type. We were radio – or, in those days, wireless – kids. Everybody was supposed to be into the Goons but it was never a particular favourite at our house. There was the adventure story Journey into Space, which was a soap opera in the stars – what will happen next on Mars? Wait till next week. More consistent for us was Radio Luxembourg from which, if one of us held a wire at the back of the radio, we got good reception. There was also the hissing, crackling and fading of the pirate station as we tried to hear the new Top Ten records. Stuart saw Patti Page on her television show singing 'How Much Is that Doggie in the Window?' and rather fancied her – his first musical influence. He was thirteen and had sneaked off to watch a neighbour's television. It was a couple of years later that Bill Haley and the Comets began the rock and roll adventure with *Rock Around the Clock*. Haley's credibility was assured in our house when he refused to appear before segregated audiences and a spokesman for the Alabama White Citizens Council declared that the aim of rock and roll was to drag down the white man to the level of the Negro: 'It is part of a plot to undermine the morals of the youth of our nation.'

But despite his agreement with Haley's attitude it was in his last year at Prescot Grammar that Stuart discovered Elvis. From that day onwards he was an Elvis fanatic. One of the first records he bought was 'Heartbreak Hotel', and his enthusiasm for that song and Presley reverberated into the lives of myself and my sister and parents. He was just *thrilled* at the buying of it, the big, black 78 rpm disc with the central blue label that he held and dusted and treated like a precious stone, a gem. While bemused critics were writing off the new voice of rock and roll as 'intellectually ridiculous', my brother was to me and my friends just being ridiculous: standing in front of a mirror, playing air guitar and noisily chorusing to the first Elvis recordings to be released in a still wobbly-legged, post-war Britain, a nation still trying to find its feet. Still, some, like Stuart, were dancing on them – well, he was shaking his hips in wild impersonation of his instant idol – enjoying what was a resurgence of life, an excitement and an opportunity.

He used to insist that Joyce and I came and listened, really listened. He told us this man was the greatest thing that ever hit the universe, and if we didn't tune in to it now we'd be sorry later on. Even my mother was drawn into the excitement over Elvis. Elvis was the god. Stuart gloried in that original Elvis 78 rpm, HMV POP 182, released in 1956, the year Stuart learned he had the qualifications for art college.

He achieved five O levels (English language and literature, geography, woodwork, and his prize, art), which was more than enough for him to get into Liverpool School of Art. In those days it literally was a doddle to get in. If you were eighteen. Stuart was two years younger and his achievement was regarded as exceptional. He was still living at home with us. He had his own room and my mother doted on him. She was a gregarious, loving woman and would have walked over oceans, fire, and king-sized beds of nails for him. My sister Joyce and I had to share a room, and I suppose were second-class citizens. Stuart's space was sacrosanct. As a marine engineer my father's career was at sea. Stuart for as long as I could remember was the man about the house. He was treated that way by my mother and took responsibilities; we all did, we grew up quickly but not fast.

The National Diploma in Design course at art school was life itself to Stuart. Even then, young as he was, he had focus and determination. It can be a curse when you really know what you want to do and achieve for the rest of life; sometimes the fun parts can hurtle past you. We officially lived outside the city, and although Stuart was guaranteed his education fees he was cut off from grants for day-to-day living. Anyway, he would not have qualified for any grant aid until he reached the normal admission age of eighteen. He didn't just miss the money but the college atmosphere. He was in an adventure, and the daily grind of getting six miles from home, on the bus with all his artwork bits and pieces, he conjured up as hideously inconvenient. In truth, he wanted to go it alone and be his own man. He had also found a friend. Stuart linked up with a fellow student, Rod Murray, to search for a studio in the city centre; it was the status thing for students to have their own place, however small and inconvenient: you were nobody in the art world unless you lived in a basement or an attic. Where you either starved or froze to death.

Rod, two years older than Stuart, had a paternal quality about him and showed Stuart the ropes. I remember Rod saying to my mother when he met her for the first time, 'Stuart only ever refers to his sisters as his little sisters. I thought they were babies and there was a huge age gap between them.' It was a reminder to me how Stuart really took the place of our father with us. Before he went to art school our treat was to be taken to the cinema on a Friday evening by our mother, and Stuart used to walk in front with Mother and we two had to walk behind. It was not just spelling out the order – it was partly because the pavements were so narrow – but still he was like a grown up. To Stuart, who had been so mollycoddled by his 'girls' at home, Rod was a man of the world. My parents weren't keen for Stuart to have a place of his own at sixteen years old. Rod's family were also hesitant and a compromise was reached – they could rent a daytime place. Stuart found a basement flat at 83 Canning Street, just round the corner from the art school in Hope Street. It comprised one long, narrow room that they used as a studio, a small kitchen with gas ring and deep, stained sink, and a freezing back room that was intended as a bedroom but was an igloo. The lavatory was outside. The woman who owned the place charged them pennies for it and allowed them to go for weeks without paying. But she was also generous to a large Irish family and allowed them to move in as well.

When the boys complained their landlady said the family were just there for a week, but it appeared permanent to the boys and Stuart came back to us. If he wanted a night out he would stay with friends but for the summer of 1957 he was at home. It was an exciting time for it was fun having a 'cool' older brother around the house again.

I was something of a teenage whiz as a hairdresser and I would cut Stuart's hair and style it with lotions and lacquer and highlight the sides. He would sit there in the bathroom smiling, with curlers and pins in his hair, looking at himself in the full-length mirror on the door. It never occurred to us that boys didn't have their hair done that way. It was all great fun and, for me, it meant more time with my brother; being four years younger is a big gap in your teens, the line between being grown up and still a kid sister is extremely hazy. When I was styling his hair we'd talk about records, about Elvis and Gene Vincent and Carl Perkins. Tommy Steele had made it in London and Lonnie Donnegan had started a skiffle craze but in Liverpool, where the first direct shipping links with New York had started, we had got used to hearing early imports of the American sounds; Ella Fitzgerald and Nat King Cole were as familiar as Arthur Askey and Tommy Handley. Kids my age wanted to be even more with it, to be hip, and the time and the place were perfect. The Teenagers were a big group and my friends were wearing jeans just like the Teenagers and dancing at the Locarno or the Grafton. At my all-girls school all the pupils' brothers wanted to be in skiffle groups, but Stuart and his friends were following the American rockers. There was lots of jiving and rocking and rolling going on. And not just at the clubs. At the cinema there was Bill Haley in *Rock Around the Clock* and Elvis in *Jailhouse Rock*. As I said, in those days you either went for Cliff Richard or Elvis, not both. We were an Elvis family – although we were also were keen on Billy Fury and Johnny Kidd and the Pirates. On Radio Luxembourg disc jockeys such as Pete Murray and Jack Jackson were playing Little Richard and Chuck Berry.

On television were series like *Cool for Cats*, *Six-Five Special* and *Oh, Boy!*. American acts touring Britain included Bill Haley and the Comets and we finally got Buddy Holly at the Liverpool Philharmonic on 20 March 1958.

Music was all around, but Stuart thought Elvis and Buddy Holly were for him to paint to. All his money went on paints and canvases and during the summer holiday of that first year at college he worked as a binman on the Liverpool Corporation rubbish-collection lorries. He didn't want the money to go out partying but to finance his art supplies. My mother would give him money for food but she finally realized it was all going into his work, which was influenced by everything: at that time on the walls at home we had five or six large, very bold paintings of scenes of Stuart working on the dustbins with the regular workmen. I'm sure Tracy Emin could interpret that. He loved that job, the team spirit of the older men. It was a lowly work holiday job but he really enjoyed it. Later, my sister and I donated a couple of these pictures to Stuart's grammar school and many, many years later they asked if they could sell them to help raise funds for a recreation complex, and we were happy to agree to that: it was a positive use of Stuart's art.

My parents, mainly my father, had seen Stuart becoming an academic or a doctor. My father was a creative artist, an excellent chess player, a fine pianist, a man with strong artistic instincts. My father didn't see anything wrong with Stuart pursuing art – but not as a job. He saw art as recreational, not vocational.

My father was away at sea when Stuart announced that he was moving out for the next year of college to a very small attic flat, 12 Canning Street. My mother was delighted about it, which surprised me. She doted on Stuart, but she clearly realized that having his own place to paint and live would make him happy. She was willing to sacrifice her time with him for that. She told Joyce and me that Stuart needed more space and more peace than he could get at home. I suspect her explanation to Joyce and me was a rehearsal of the argument she would give my father; he knew my mother was capable of deciding matters on her own, but I'm sure it made him feel alienated.

Rod Murray stayed at the flat with Stuart occasionally. It was right at the top, a tiny little room, an easel and a couple of dozen paintings and a bed. My mother used to drag Joyce or me around there once a week to exchange Stuart's dirty washing for a freshly laundered bundle. By then she knew his money was going into his paintings, so we would bring food with us rather than leave money for it and my mother also paid the milkman herself. That autumn in 1957 was an important time for Stuart and, indeed, for us all. Stuart had his independence. And John Lennon started at his art school. Although John was a year below Stuart they became instant *compadres* for, despite their shared short-sightedness, they spotted each other immediately, an eccentric couple but a couple nevertheless. I think there was someone, somewhere, with blue touchpaper. For, in time, John changed all our lives.

two

First Loves

'He was like a fellow who'd been born without brakes.'

Tutor Philip Hartas on John Lennon

project for plaster and copperwire

MY MOTHER AND I met the red-nosed milkman first. And then John Lennon. I still can't decide which one was more animated. The milkman always seemed to be at Stuart's flat when we visited. We thought he was radar-controlled. Also, he always wanted two or three weeks' money although it seemed he had just been paid the week before. I always wondered if he was in with Stuart to get more cash out of my mother. It wouldn't have surprised me, for in early 1958 Stuart was always short of cash.

My mother and I were wandering home along Hope Street that afternoon when we bumped into John and Stuart who were about to cross the road to the Philharmonic pub. We'd heard about John from Stuart but it was the first time my mother or I had met him. He seemed shy and had no casual conversation. I immediately felt intimidated by him. On being introduced he hardly made eye contact, barely acknowledged us at all. He appeared not to conform to bourgeois conventions like saying, 'Hello' or 'Pleased to meet you.'

He was interestingly dressed. He was neither a Teddy boy nor a beatnik, a hybrid. I liked how he looked. Stuart was clearly very proud of him. Stuart was lean and not very tall, around five feet seven, but people always looked at him, picked him out. He wore these tight jeans and coloured shirts. And his dark glasses on his freckled face. They were part of his uniform long before he left

Liverpool. I suspect that many of John's actions reflected some of my brother's rebellious inner wishes. In that way they were committed to each other, a team: John was mesmerized by Stuart, who was always a noted stylist, crossing the boundaries between high and low art. Our first meeting with John made it obvious that being different was a quality much admired by Stuart.

John was scruffy in attitude but not in the intriguing way he looked. The beatnik phase was tired but still around and John had hints of it along with the winkle-pickers and drainpipe jeans – drainies – and greasy hair in what we called a Tony Curtis style, a ludicrous, gravity-defying endeavour involving jars of Brylcreem. He kept looking at Stuart who was talking to us but was unusually nervous. John was bigger than my brother and was quiet, but like a firework; I felt his personality could explode.

My mother was chatty, wanting to know the latest news from Stuart. She also wanted to take a measure of her son's friend. John was little more than a toddler when his father Fred Lennon, an orphan and merchant seaman, vanished from home and left him with his mother Julia, who was always joking and had a grand smile. He was brought up mainly by his aunt, Mimi Smith, who shared his mother's looks but not her personality. She was strict with him. His mother would let him get away with anything but Aunt Mimi was always particular. She *looked* frightening to us kids. She had a strong jaw and wore a hat and was stern in appearance. She didn't seem to have much humour about her. She was very direct in her approach to my mother when she was clearly finding out who we were, checking that Stuart was good enough for John to be associating with. With hindsight I think she was a bit of a snob, but so was John. When I first met her she had lost her husband and her sister within a few a years of each other, and she may have been hiding a lot of distress. She certainly did not seem to be coping well with John. That is how I see it all these years later: at the time, for us youngsters, she was a forbidding figure, like the Wicked Witch from *The Wizard of Oz*.

She loved John more than anything, and had done since the moment she saw him half an hour after he was born at the maternity hospital in Oxford Street, Liverpool. It's part of the legend now that John Winston Lennon was born during a bellow of an air raid at 6.29 p.m. on 9 October 1940. It was Mimi who called him John. His mother, forgivably, given the timing of her son's arrival, favoured Winston. Sense and patriotism both got their way which, with hindsight, was appropriate for a baby destined to always be pulled in different directions. Stuart was born after a twenty-hour labour at the Simpson Maternity Hospital in Edinburgh, a few months earlier, on 23 June. My mother was tiny, only five feet tall, so the birth of each of us was prolonged and later she had ongoing medical problems. Although Stuart and John both had sailor fathers, their beginnings could not have been more different.

John had been raised as an only child by Julia, her sister Mimi and Mimi's husband George. Freddy Lennon had left Julia with her baby son. It was natural for Mimi and George, who had no children of their own, to want to help out. Julia continued to live nearby, and often visited John at her sister's home. They remained in close and frequent contact, although Julia later had more children. Julia totally handed over the immediate care of John to Mimi when John was five years old; John would resent this, feel rejected, but he and his mother became friends as the years went on. As a teenager John was a rascal and Julia would let him get away with anything; while Mimi in her semi-detached house in Woolton was lecturing him against smoking and drinking, Julia, who was living across town with her new family, would be offering him a cigarette. John was a man without any real infrastructure throughout his life, no control, and the way he always was all goes back to this time.

His natural mother, Julia, had not intended to abandon him when, owing to her circumstances, she accepted her sister Mimi's offer to raise John with her husband George; no rejection was intended, but it is often severely felt by little ones. Julia taught him to play the banjo, didn't care whether he was off school or not, and then he'd go home to Mimi who had rules. None of that helped his normal development – playing by the rules one moment, a rebel the next. We had all believed that George owned a dairy, and their lifestyle in Menlove Avenue supported that; it was a part of town regarded as an upmarket area. It was only later that it transpired that he had only worked for the dairy.

In 1955, John's family was devastated by the sudden and premature death of George, John's surrogate father, who suffered a brain haemorrhage, and three years later by the death of Julia. What was even more tragic was that he had really become very close to his mother when she was knocked down by a police car and killed. It happened in the evening of 15 July 1958, when Julia was leaving Menlove Avenue to return to her own home. She was on her way to catch a bus. Stuart was so upset for John, but said that John had not said much about it. He'd cursed and shouted but had not cried. But he said John had changed overnight from the student he had met only nine months earlier. By then Stuart and John could talk for hours about anything, but Stuart said Julia's death was some-thing that John needed to keep to himself. I think his demeanour was his pain protection. With George's death Mimi became, in effect, a single parent. John was only seventeen when Julia died: he was an angry, rebellious young man, who often cut classes and mocked authority figures. Clearly, the extremes of John's personality were formed before his mother's death and before he met Stuart nine months earlier. A thread that runs through their relationship is that John respected Stuart, took notice of him. John said he looked up to Stuart, who always told him the truth. That shows a quality in John that I think is quite special; that he was aware at some level of what he was missing, what he hadn't had enough of, and knew how to source it to some extent. One of the really smart things in life is to know how to get some of the gaps filled in. Stuart was the conduit for that information, and that led to a deep relationship between them.

Young John was juggling all these demons when he joined Liverpool School of Art in September 1957. By happy chance, Stuart was by then a member of the Students' Union committee and involved in organizing all the college dances. He was also getting a reputation as an artist to watch. Arthur Ballard, who was a tutor at the college, was friendly with my father and kept a kind eye on Stuart, but when he realized Stuart had a gift he took even more interest. He said he found Stuart's work inventive and very curious, which are important instincts in an artist. Arthur would sit and sip his whisky and watch Stuart paint for hours and hours, conducting his tutorials in Stuart's flat; his idea was, why disrupt an artist at work? He was truly a fan, admiring the artist in the body of such a young man. It was Bill Harry, a friend of Stuart's, who introduced him to the new boy at college, John Lennon.

John might as well have worn a sandwich board announcing the end of the world, so clearly was he dressed for attention. His jeans were the tightest anywhere – he only got out of Mimi's house by wearing a pair of flannels over them, taking them off on his way to college and shoving them in a shoulder bag – and he had a long, frocked black jacket, like a Mississippi gambler. He wore it all with a swagger, with self-assurance camouflaging all his insecurities. Stuart, who adopted his own individual style, dressed for himself – who but a few intimates would see his red underpants? Stuart was impressed by him, and even more so when he heard about John's group, the Quarrymen, named after the Quarry Bank High School that John and the original band members had attended. But the band was not the main attraction. John was overtly anarchic, whereas Stuart's anarchy was expressed by pushing artistic boundaries, painting large works when he should have been doing small-scale material. Stuart's rebellion was mostly acceptable, whereas John's sometimes wasn't. We are all shocked and appalled by wild behaviour, but we are also excited and fascinated by it. John was also *very, very* funny. Stuart loved that and could keep up with it. There was a lot of banter between them, each of them always trying to get the better line. Once, round at our house, John said to me, 'You know, your brother's a little genius.' I got back quickly, 'He thinks you're a big genius.' His smile embraced me.

John was also very dangerous, and there is a kind of excitement about that too. That unpredictability. In their banter John could be very cruel but, like a strong parent, Stuart contained that, which also made John feel safe.

At first John was selfish with their friendship; he kept Stuart to himself, though he sometimes included Bill Harry; they would escape to the Cracke, a pub near the college, where they moaned about their lectures, talked Buddy Holly, Elvis and rock and roll, and fumbled for the loose change to buy beer and Woodbine cigarettes. Doris, the landlady, regularly used to ban John but he would soon charm his way back. Bill Harry said that John's out-landish, extrovert sort of genius was a significant factor in his attraction for and to Stuart; that John liked and wanted strong personalities and he learned from Stuart a certain mystic quality. He said Stuart was different from other people, and that attracted John. He also admitted that John could be very cruel and that Stuart was an obvious target, but said that Stuart had an extraordinary resilience, for John also loved Stuart. Stuart had also proven himself to John – he could be pushed, but not pushed away.

It is interesting for me to talk to Stuart's friends from so long ago, and their memories are helpful: I certainly was not with my brother for every minute of his life. What is also fascinating is how their reaction to Stuart and John is like my own; most people wanted to mother or look after Stuart, but John initially made you lean back from him, look for cover. Jean Francis, who was in the year above Stuart, said she was shy and lonely at college and Stuart was one of the few boys who befriended her. Jean said she found John quite alarming and kept well out of his way. She remembers an incident related to her by one of the college's life models. The tutor was out of the room and John told a joke. Everyone thought it was very funny and they all laughed. But John just stood there unsmiling and stared at them, and gradually the laughter faded and everyone became embarrassed.

It was around this time that Cynthia Powell, who would become Cynthia Lennon and my friend, met Stuart. Cynthia was, at first, a twin-set girl, an art student from Hoylake, across the water. I hate the word, but posh best describes John's first impressions of Cynthia. He was clearly attracted to her but hid that behind a regular barrage of bad jokes about her. She was the most important person to him for a long time but John did not want to look weak to his peers, to be soppy over a girl. Cynthia and Stuart got on much better, and Cynthia has told me many times how people at college couldn't help being aware of Stuart; she said he could always be found at work, always sketching something. She said it was clear to everyone that art was his whole life. By the time Cynthia began going out with John they were both good friends of my brother. When John was difficult with either of them they also had each other; Cynthia said she was so close to Stuart she instinctively turned to him, and he her, when John's moods became too difficult to cope with alone. She also emphasized that John and Stuart had a remarkable affinity, each transmitting his own particular talents to the other.

Arthur Ballard always said he felt that Stuart was more John's mentor than his best friend. He said they both had their own friends in college, apart from each other. John was the heavy drinker, the raver, and Arthur called him a bloody nuisance in pubs. He never could recall Stuart ever being out of step in that way, but he might have just been considerate to us after Stuart's death. He was a red-blooded boy and must have let himself go now and again. Nevertheless, Arthur said you couldn't ignore Stuart as there was something very beguiling about him; he saw Stuart as a wistful yet tough character. He totally believed that Stuart nurtured in John a desire to learn more. One example he gave was about the Dada movement – art is mindless – that began in Switzerland during the First World War as a reaction to the awful casualties of that conflict.

The later Beatles films had broad brush strokes of Dadaist humour, but Arthur said John wouldn't have known Dada from a donkey without Stuart.

Philip Hartas was more understanding of John when he knew of his childhood, but he still thought that his student with no brakes ran over a lot of people. It upset him to see the way John switched from being charming and charismatic to being cruel and hurtful. Again, it is all part of the big picture. John was called a romantic gone sour, but maybe all along he was a sour romantic. These young men were growing up and it was a difficult time for them but John and Stuart, though poles apart, were magnetically handcuffed. John did not like to be seen as keen to learn, but he wanted to. He would try not to appear to be interested in studies, but after class would insist that Stuart taught him painting techniques. Cynthia, who by 1958 was very much John's girlfriend (she was pregnant with Julian when they married on 23 August 1962), would be ordered to wait in a corner until these private lessons were over. Stuart helped him through his intermediate exams and to transfer his skills from lettering to painting. He also got him going about lectures, about theory, about understanding. I suppose it was all about trying to make John understand. However, it was not all one-way traffic: Stuart was intrigued by John too. And John could make everyone laugh, pronouncing of one of Stuart's long-worked-on abstracts that hanging was too good for it. That was John in good humour. There was also lots of the other sort but they bickered like brothers, not competitors.

My brother and John were each side of the same coin. They sparked off one another rather than becoming like clones. Yet, at times, they would walk, talk and dress the same and even flick their cigarette ash with similar, calculated disdain but they never lost their separate individuality. Stuart certainly acted as if he was in a French movie. They were like schoolboys smoking Gauloises behind the school bicycle sheds – not enjoying it, but for some demented reason needing to do it. They would wander around the college campus and be in heated debate, with John the most animated, waving his arms in the air, always loud, reflecting his stature and personality. He went through college like King Kong. There was much debris. By comparison, Stuart was skinny, introverted because of his focus on work and, because he was so intense, appeared remote to some people. With his little scowl and fine bone structure he was a face, the flickering black-and-white Movietone image of the archetypal 1950s hero. People have always said he looked like James Dean, but I have never seen it quite that way; maybe I am too close. I think he was unique, and he looks like it to me every day when I walk past a framed portrait of him that hangs in the hallway of my home in west London. It's not some morbid fascination, he's next to the bathroom. I see him regularly, with his cigarette and his guitar and his beloved boots, and it is Stuart, not someone else's ghost. When Stuart was at art college the young were escaping from wartime heroes – John Winston was always a reminder of one – and creating their own, often overnight. At times, it was a game to find characters, new and from the past, who they would consider worthy of their adulation, and it seemed that the more obscure your choice, the cooler you were.

For the art students there were other grand figures to discuss now – not just Elvis and Gene Vincent who were such big role models for most late 1950s teenage boys. Heroes were painters like Amedeo Modigliani, the Italian artist whose fascination was as much about his lifestyle as his work: Modigliani's short life was punctuated by alcoholic binges that culminated in a permanent blackout. Another admired figure was the dissipated French poet Arthur Rimbaud whose teenage achievements vanished in a life of drink and drugs. Rimbaud never goes out of fashion. Leonardo DiCaprio played the 'Messiah' of poetry in the 1996 film *Total Eclipse*, and a 2001 biography, *Rimbaud*, by Graham Robb was shortlisted for the Samuel Johnson Prize. It was the starving-artist-dying-young-for-his-art fantasy that appealed to many, but I don't think Stuart and John were ever the true starving-in-a-garret types;

Stuart was too enthralled with his work, then enamoured by the Pre-Raphaelites, and John with his group the Quarrymen who in 1957 became a seven-musician line-up when Paul McCartney joined. John's art studies suffered because of his drive and time with the Quarrymen, but Stuart was always helping him get back up to standard and fill out his notebooks with the required research notes and essays. They had really become best friends when in wintry 1957 Stuart and Rod Murray moved from Canning Street to another place that was still within easy walking distance of the college; there was a small snag – it was exclusively for a single person. Stuart was the tenant and Rod became the artful lodger. The new flat was a back room on the middle floor of 9 Percy Street, Liverpool 8. Although, possibly, not yet as famous an address as Penny Lane or Abbey Road on the Beatle trail, it was where Stuart and John Lennon were to make their first recordings together.

three

Percy Street

'What've you got?'

Marlon Brando, in response to being asked what
he is rebelling against in *The Wild One*, 1954

STUART'S PERCY STREET landlady, the formidable Mrs Plant, was an antique dealer who owned several other properties in the street and lived in Number 3. Stuart's new place was a treasure of Victorian furniture including intimidating sideboards with bevelled mirrors and white, true marble fireplaces. The boys were not amused. They decided to paint their room white and dismantle the large fireplace and smuggle the pieces out. Stuart painted everything in the flat, the furniture and walls in his room, with black and white spots and stripes in what was artistic experimenting, not interior design. What a mess it was, with canvases and newspapers and paints all over the place. They also found a stash of old furniture which without thinking they broke up for firewood. Mostly, it comprised antique pieces to be repaired or restored. Mrs Plant was kept at bay by the rent always being delivered on time, directly to her. They did not want any knocking on the door of Number 9, no cosy cups of tea with Mrs Plant. Percy Street became a fun place for Stuart and his friends – and the location for some of Stuart and John Lennon's first recordings. Stuart bought a cheap record player when he moved in, and what was left over went on rock and roll records. He was the first to buy every Elvis single available, but 'Heartbreak Hotel' remained a favourite. He liked Ray Charles, and I think that was because of the layers of Charles's music; Stuart could dig into it. It was Rod Murray who became Stuart and John's record producer. In a live-now-pay-later moment he had bought a tape recorder, forging Arthur Ballard's signature as guarantor of the arrangement. That deceit was soon forgotten as they made their recordings – everything from taking off the Goons – (John was Peter Sellers, skinny Stuart was Harry Secombe, Rod was Michael Bentine and Spike Milligan) to doing Elvis songs. Some nights, after sessions at the Cracke, John and Stuart would sing and record Elvis and Gene Vincent numbers late into the night. I wonder where those tapes, a remarkable archive, are now. The Quarrymen would also rehearse at Percy Street, which may not have impressed the neighbours but would most certainly music scholars and enthusiasts today. Rod Murray and some of the others were really into skiffle; Rod had made his own washboard and along with Stuart they would all jam together, singing and playing improvised instruments, with the Quarrymen.

Rod Murray, the kindest of men, landed in trouble for helping to create a moment of popular history. He missed some payments on the tape recorder and the mighty Ballard, a substantial person to upset, was alerted by the hire purchase company. The boys were lucky to solve the problem. Stuart and Rod were both on the Students' Union entertainment committee, and the Union bought the machine outright and Rod out of the mess. The tapes? Rod says they were simply lost, but such things always turn up sometime and we shall see. I have witnessed so many lost recordings appear over the years that I never say never. The recordings and the company added to the atmosphere of Percy Street. John would stay for a time and then go back to Aunt Mimi for some coddling and feeding-up. Cynthia was around, and she and John were becoming more and more a very established couple. Stuart was also attracting girls. He was also still reading, wanting to learn more all the time. It would get on Rod's nerves, for the lights never went out at Number 9. Stuart would be painting or reading, Hemingway, Steinbeck, Stendhal, and, I was to find out, *The Kama Sutra*. Apparently he wanted the theory as well as the steady procession of young ladies through the flat. He was always a perfectionist, wanted to get it right. Stuart was also the romantic artist and when he really liked a girl he would go to work; he did hundreds of drawings and paintings of one girl he went out with for several months. She had that longish-neck look favoured by Modigliani. I'm not sure, but was that sex impersonating life and imitating art or vice versa? Whatever. I'm sure none of them cared too much. I think most people can understand what was going on: there were lots of hormones in a hurry. Another girl would catch Stuart's eye and he would paint her – painting over the other girls' canvases possibly to cover up memories but certainly to save money. Cash flow was always a difficulty. Which was where John the Drunk was a bonus.

The downstairs flat in Percy Street, two rooms and a kitchen, was taken over by a man called John. He had income from somewhere but spent his time jumping into the bottle and pulling the cork in after him. In a rare sober moment, he asked Stuart and Rod if they would consider preparing their evening meal for three people instead of just two and leave a portion for him in his kitchen. For this service he would pay them half a crown a day. They agreed on a good deal, but soon it became better. After 10 p.m., pub closing time, John would stagger home and collapse in the hall and Stuart and Rod would go down and manoeuvre him into bed. He never touched the food they had left. They stopped leaving the food but kept charging. John never noticed.

In fact, he was so happy with the arrangement that Rod became, for one pound sterling a week, his tenant, all approved by Mrs Plant. What she didn't see was the wardrobe split between Stuart and Rod. There was only one wardrobe, so in a Musketeer gesture they literally split it 50–50, cut it in half and painted one part black, the other white. The criterion was to be stylish – in whatever you were involved with. Then, being a Liverpudlian meant, by definition, being trendy. Everything and everyone from Merseyside was exciting. There were more than 300 Merseyside rock groups, the Mersey beat was everywhere. Rock was rapidly overtaking skiffle as the most popular music, and big attractions included the Searchers, the Undertakers, the Merseybeats, Faron's Flamingos and the Swinging Blue Jeans.

We seemed to be living at the centre of the world, albeit a small world: the Jacaranda coffee bar was the social mecca. It was where the students and the office girls went, where people clicked. The clubs were also changing. The local strict-tempo dancing palais were still popular, but we teenagers were still struggling to find our own music. Alan Sytner ran jazz nights at the Temple restaurant in the city but didn't enjoy the ambience. He found what he wanted at a club called Le Caveau by the Seine in Paris. He decided to re-create it in the basement at 10 Matthew Street near the Liverpool city centre and called it the Cavern Club. What had been a wartime air-raid shelter and then a wine cellar was in 1956 being used to store electrical equipment. Literally downmarket Matthew Street, home to tall, crumbly Victorian warehouses and fruit and vegetable lorries, was in for a shock. A loud one. On 16 January 1957, the Cavern opened to the sound of the Merseysippi Jazz Band. The club was jammed with 600 people – about another 1,500 lined up but failed to get in.

The Cavern was turned into a car park in the 1980s by Liverpool City Council, apparently blindly unaware of the economics of nostalgia. In 1957 John played there with the Quarrymen, but I had to wait another couple of years to see my brother there as a Beatle and that was before I became a regular at the doorway, which was lighted by one bare bulb; eighteen stone steps went down into the black-painted cellar, which was split into three areas by archways. It was a bubble of smoke, sweat, bad lavatories, no air conditioning, condensation, and dancing and the music everyone wanted to hear. It was a template for British clubs of the sixties – hell holes fans fought and paid to get into. Along with them, I loved it. As would Paul McCartney. He had joined the Quarrymen in July 1957, after meeting John at an open-air performance at St Peter's Church fête at Woolton. That year he was a pupil at the Liverpool Institute, a grammar school next door to the art school, and doing his A levels. A year younger than Paul, George Harrison was also a pupil there but one more interested in music than his O levels.

Paul was always smiling and friendly, and over the years many people have wondered why and how anybody could be so nice; that has always been his style. In those early days he would usually sit with John and Stuart in the college canteen at lunchtime. He was just sixteen years old, so the older boys were a little impressive. Paul has often said that he was the working-class kid whereas John and Stuart were middle class. John, Paul argued, had an aunt called Harriet and relatives who were dentists or worked at the BBC. The clincher was that one of John's uncles was Paul's English teacher at the institute. He said he got a better education from John and Stuart, who led him into a world of poetry, beatniks, Bohemians and art school parties. At his home books and symphony music were not daily items; Paul said that at that time his vision of such life was from television. What must it have been like for him to see John and Stuart messing around and quoting beat poets and showing off intimate knowledge of art and artists? Later, Paul would take up painting himself. For the moment he was intent on making his mark with the Quarrymen, who were a hugely talented bunch.

By the end of Stuart's summer term in 1958, George Harrison had joined the Quarrymen line-up. Every day he shared a bus to the Institute with Paul and talked the older lad into getting him in, arguing that his guitar expertise compensated for his youth. George got frustrated by the lack of play dates and tried to join Rory Storm and the Hurricanes, but they rejected him as too young. What a lucky lad he was. He stayed with John and Paul and within a year George had a Hofner President guitar, which was very smart for a sixteen-year-old. Stuart heard all the rock and roll gossip from John but at that time, at an end-of-term party on the top floor of the college, he met Susan Williams, a first-year fashion design student. He spent the evening teaching her to jive but, like Cinderella, she had to leave and was lost for a time. Stuart got lost in his work. He had become a painting student and was doing a series of five-foot by three-foot, big, abstract paintings, mixing sand with his oil paints and using big brushes to create giant machine type shapes, loosely painted but very strong. Stuart worked with Charles Burton, the head of the Painting School, who told me he thought Stuart was a great guy with tremendous energy. He said he once asked Stuart to produce a painting of a wall, and told him to go out and just look at the surface of a wall first. Moments later Stuart, so carried away with enthusiasm, raced back to say he had seen a wall. Burton was taken by the eagerness. He said he also tried to point Stuart in the direction of his favourite music, jazz, and especially Louis Armstrong. Stuart, he said, told him with a smile, 'We think Elvis is the boy.' Stuart gave his tutor two Elvis records and more than three decades later Charles Burton still had them. Stuart, or maybe it was Elvis, certainly made an impression. I like to think it was a combination of the two. I dismissed the thought long ago that people were just being considerate of my feelings when it came to talking about Stuart. He died a long time ago and you never place a halo, confer sainthood, on family, for you learn it is more important to be loving and fair. I have found through my life and my work that to be direct with your opinions is better than to tease, to half-agree or halfheartedly argue. Professionally, I know when people are holding back or attempting to shade their opinions. What I have found is that those who were around Stuart are open, as he was, and although their hairstyles may have changed, vanished in some cases, their memories are intact.

I have been told many inspiring stories about Stuart and his time at Liverpool School of Art. I think he was content with his work because it was going well. There's nothing better for making you feel good than knowing you are achieving something, getting somewhere. June Furlong, a college life model, can say she posed for Augustus John – and my brother. She says she was Stuart's favourite model and remembers his energy and draughtsmanship. He liked to draw her, she says, with her hands behind her back. She even remembers where at the college: Room 701.

Heartening to our family, and especially to me who has taken such an interest in art and been involved with a London gallery, the Liverpool art legend Arthur Ballard had little sympathy with the view held by some of Stuart's tutors that he was running before he could walk. He disdained their argument that Stuart had moved on too quickly, saying that Stuart was one of the most creative and original students he had experienced in fifty years of teaching. He said he had met students who were more competent than Stuart in the disciplines and techniques but few, if any, had that spark that is genius. It was astonishing praise for such a young artist. Arthur was so overtaken by Stuart's abilities that he said he forgot he was a student and regarded him as a fellow artist. Arthur would go and watch Stuart paint and then they would go to the Cracke and analyse the work. But Stuart's thoughts were clearly not far away from John, for he attempted to write a novel – I still have some pages of it – in which the central character, John, who also appears as Nhoke, is an artist living in horrid rooms in Puke Street. It is, in its way, stuttering satire. It is also heartbreaking, for Stuart writes of the terrible change in John/Nhoke nine months after they met, in time and incident that mirror the death of John's mother Julia. He also conjures up an early portrait of John and, of course, himself, writing of his hero: 'He was capricious, incalculable and self-centred, yet at the same time he was always a loyal friend. A frustrated and misunderstood child not given its due need of affection, ends as a man without roots, in rebellion or bewilderment, almost embittered, this was John. Painting had reached the point of obsession with him. He lived it, ate, slept and drank it.'

Stuart was not too serious. He still had Elvis, and 'Teddy Bear' was his favourite record at the time. Susan Williams told me this for, without need of glass slipper, she was once again in Stuart's life.

Fittingly, it was spring 1959; we were all on the cusp of the sixties, and I swear few could have ever predicted the social revolution that was to follow, that we were indeed to be all shook up. We had no idea. Susan became a regular visitor at Percy Street and remembers that Stuart's room was full of college easels. His dress style was as colourful as his room and work, and that flair was not too constrained by his meagre funds. Susan says she went round Lewis's department store with him once in the search for red underpants, which were very hard to find in those days. His socks had to be red too. And he had a pair of pink-striped jeans that he used to wear with a short black T-shirt. Susan never saw Stuart as a Beatle, one of the very few Liverpudlians of her generation who never saw the group perform in any of their several incarnations. She had to work in the evenings to support herself, and also had to babysit in return for her lodgings. Stuart often babysat with her. Her college teaching group included John and Cynthia, to whom she was close. Susan felt John was aspiring to Cynthia, this respectable, very nice girl; she was also convinced that Cynthia only tolerated John's bad behaviour because she was totally in love with him. Susan saw that other side of John on a college bus trip to see a Picasso exhibition in London. Stuart, who couldn't afford the trip, was to have hidden under Susan's seat, but the girl in the next seat was a member of the organizing committee and threw him off the bus. Angry and upset, Susan moved to a seat next to another of their class, Rod Jones. John suddenly, unreasonably, went bananas. He shouted abuse at Susan and she gave him some back, criticizing the way he treated women. Susan laughs at it now: she and John screaming at each other and all the rest of the bus relishing every moment of the row.

The romance between Stuart and Susan ended as it had begun, at a college party, for which he had drawn tremendous murals. They had arranged to meet there, but when Susan arrived there was no sign of him and so she danced with Rod Murray. Later, she saw Stuart dancing with another girl, and left to go to another party without him. His explanation a week later was that he'd arrived late and seen Susan dancing with Rod, and as they appeared to be getting on well he found another girl. It had not been kismet for either of them. But destiny was plotting elsewhere at Liverpool School of Art – in the basement.

The Quarrymen regularly rehearsed in one of the college's Life rooms and performed in the basement, between trad-jazz sessions. George Harrison, as the young lad, was always making overtures to John, trying to impress him. It made John more aloof – he did not want to be seen to be taking the younger boy seriously. Nevertheless, George was more of a rebel, like John, than Paul or Stuart were. Paul and George openly resented how close and arty John and Stuart were. For them, Stuart would always be a gooseberry in their relationship. Stuart and John were the big boys. They shared rooms, they were students, not grammar school pupils, they were artists, and they were clever and funny, always bouncing lines off each other. It was as if they were in a secret society. Paul and George felt shut out and their subliminal anger would manifest itself in nasty remarks, in put-downs. Stuart and John were so close they might as well have been standing together in the band.

Stuart had a new girlfriend, Veronica Johnson, and she was not in the least impressed by these particular Quarrymen, John, Paul, and George – and forgotten man Ken Brown. Ken, however, was vitally important at this moment; he was a friend of Pete Best, and Pete's mother Mona ran the Casbah, a new social club for teenagers in Hayman's Green, West Derby. Mona Best ran the Casbah in the basement of her large Victorian home and needed a Saturday-night group; Ken suggested the Quarrymen, and for seven consecutive Saturday nights until the middle of October 1959 the Quarrymen played their first regular and professional bookings. They were paid three pounds an evening – between them; they would have played for a shared cup of tea. Success breeds success, no matter how small the beginnings. After their Casbah run they became the official Liverpool Art School band and, as such, Stuart, who was spending much of his time with the group, believed the Students' Union committee was justified in buying them amplification equipment – which made the rehearsals at Percy Street a little more lively for the neighbours.

They weren't so animated when they came round to our house. When Stuart was playing with the Beatles they were round all the time, but even before that one or other of them would call round to pick him up for a night out. There was always something going on – a new group, a new rival, to see, another club opening to attend. Their lives did not revolve around Saturday nights out – every night was an opportunity to go somewhere.

We saw Paul but more of George and John, from time to time; they were on their best behaviour with my mother. I liked Paul, much to my brother's dismay. I was a young teen and he was not as powerful or as charismatic, as frightening, as John and he was closer to my age and sort of pretty. He was not so much a challenge as John. I always regarded George as a bit too young and a bit too scruffy. But he and my mother got on so well together. He would walk in and instantly say, 'Hello, Mrs Sutcliffe, how are you?' My mother would have the kettle on before he'd finished that sentence. George was always the chatty one with all of us. Paul was a little bit more awkward with Joyce and me but he got on with my mother. They were friends of Stuart's and she went out of her way to be pleasant to them; her motives may have been to find out as much as possible about the boys her son was going out with. They were a group of boys, a gang in the best sense, before they ever were a band. But John and Stuart were top dogs and that was always a problem for Paul and George, for they did not feel totally included in everything that was happening. At our home they were included by my mother and always warmly welcomed. But no matter how glad my mother said she was to see him, John was John. He had his moments and would make my mother laugh, but normally he was reluctant to engage with us and I just thought he was socially gauche.

On reflection, I think it was still some unrealized anti-establishment feeling because we looked quite grand compared with them.

We were in our mansion flat in Sefton Park, which is where they used to come to visit us. It's all relative. In Liverpool terms we looked the very middle class with taste. We had art. We had a good piano. We had books. My parents were both educated with professional jobs. Although John would also be regarded as middle class compared with the other Beatles-to-be, we looked a bit better. It's interesting, because Paul's mother was a district midwife, which in those days was a very respectable job. She always wanted the very best for her boys. His father was an administrator at the Cotton Exchange. He wasn't digging holes in the road. He wasn't blue-collar. The truly working-class one was George. But I liked his mother very much. I thought she was a very nice woman. Whenever Paul came to our house, he'd either read a magazine or play the piano, but do his best not to talk to us. So much so, that the feeling I got at the time was that he used it like a waiting room. The most social was George. The youngest, he appeared the most comfortable with us. As I said, he was the one that my mother paid most attention to; she was always asking if he was hungry. My mother almost needed a route map to the kitchen. She could do it, could cook well, but she just preferred to either do her stint of work for school or mark books, but she used to go to the kitchen to make him a sandwich or some tea. If John was there to pick him up he and Stuart would be talking art and rock records – that was what Stuart's life revolved around.

A distinguished sculptor and Royal Academician, Mike Kenny, who with his wife Susan was a very close friend of mine, witnessed that. Sadly, he died at the end of 1999. Forty years earlier he attended the college and teamed up with Stuart and John and was soon a regular at 9 Percy Street. He told me that on one visit Stuart had just bought a new Everly Brothers record and obsessively played it over and over all evening. He said Stuart was the same about work, swiftly creating abstract sculptures and paintings. Of course, I was used to Stuart working to Elvis records, but that seemed to impress Mike and the other students. Stuart's work, I might venture, really was Pop Art. Yet he was so serious that often he was not as kind as he might have been with others who he felt were not, as they say today, on message. Stuart's vision was that the making of art is a thinking activity.

By late 1959 Ken Brown had left the Quarrymen and John, Paul and George had a new incarnation: they were Johnny and the Moondogs. While the Moondogs made music, Stuart went to work on a great big abstract expressionist painting to submit for the prestigious biennial John Moores Exhibition to be held at the Walker Gallery; it was eight feet by eight feet in two pieces of eight feet by four feet. When it was completed Stuart and Rod Murray carried the first half down to the gallery and then went for a drink to get over their exertions. They planned to take the other half the following day, but Mrs Plant, their landlady, entered the frame. Rod was asleep, suffering from a late party, when Mrs Plant prodded him in the ribs: he saw the blue stockings first, and said he was praying he had not slept with this woman who was behaving more and more like a banshee. She told the befuddled Rod it was 10 a.m. and he thought that was nice, his landlady telling him the time. Then she ordered him out of the flat by noon. He thought this totally unreasonable until his mind focused and he saw one of Mrs Plant's antique chairs smouldering in the fireplace. Mrs Plant went through the rest of the building like a bulldozer, stumbling over broken rules and furniture. The reaction was swift and clear – everybody out. Stuart came home for a week or so and that was nice for my mother, who always had his room ready, Joyce and me, but he was clearly anxious to find another place of his own. This he did quite quickly, and it was not long before John Lennon moved in too. He would make Stuart an offer – typically, off the top of his head – that would begin one of the most amazing stories of popular history.

four

The Blonde

'Generally, we got on quite well but there were moments,
definitely, when it was me and Stuart head to head.'

Paul McCartney

STUART AND ROD Murray moved closer to the college, to three rooms in Flat 3 Hillary Mansions, in Gambier Terrace. The rent was three pounds a week and great value for the space, which was just as well as lots of people were going to fill it. Rod Murray's girlfriend moved into one front room, Rod had the other, and Stuart took the enormous back room. Before long, Rod moved in with his girlfriend and Rod Jones took over the smaller front room and John moved in with Stuart. Cynthia was to spend a lot of time in Stuart's room.

I remember it as quite pleasant, but she had a totally different impression. She remembers a double mattress under a dirty, curtain-less window, canvases and half-squeezed tubes of oil paint all over the place and paint splashed about the wooden floor; I don't remember the empty chip papers in the sooty fireplace, but she does and she was there more than I was. And there were more and more visitors, with George and Paul tipping up to chat and rehearse. I suppose squalor builds up, like greasy floors, and, like beauty, is in the eye of the beholder. I have to admit there was a touch of dampness about the place and that even the communal bathroom was converted to sleeping quarters for overnight guests, which must have led to some interesting situations during the wee hours. I have photographs of the flats in Percy Street and Gambier Terrace and they look quite smart to me, but you would smarten up for a photographer, wouldn't you? All Stuart had vision for was his work, and all over the walls were posters and charcoal sketches, mostly nudes of Stuart's favourite life-class model June Furlong. Cynthia said that when she visited John – it was where they consummated their relationship – it was clear that Stuart wanted nothing more than to be allowed to get on with his work (although by then his interest in music was overlapping from listening to it to making it). He never liked being an onlooker, as he was with the band; the catch-22 was that he could not play an instrument, so how could he show he was qualified to play? John was more and more aware of that, and they talked into the night about it when Stuart's arms ached so much he could paint no more. The second half of Stuart's painting for the John Moores Exhibition never made it to the Walker Gallery. Months later my mother and sister and I collected it from the Gambier Terrace backyard where it had sat unprotected in all weathers. Happily, the first half, titled *Summer Painting*, was the only student work accepted for the exhibition. That happpenstance helped give birth to the Beatles.

Summer Painting was bought by the exhibition's benefactor, John Moores. He was part of the Liverpool dynasty connected to the Littlewoods football pools organization and a wonderful philanthropist. He paid sixty-five pounds for it, an impressive amount of money for someone paying a share of three pounds a week in rent. John was with Stuart when he was told that his painting had been sold. John gave Stuart his regular artistic line: 'And I didn't think it was fit for hangin'.'

The solidly built Arthur Ballard – there was a hint of Bob Hoskins menace about him – went to the opening of the exhibition and, not surprisingly, on to the Cracke pub afterwards. He overheard a group of students criticising the remarks Stuart made when he received his cheque from John Moores. He loudly defended Stuart to them and then went off to the lavatory. As he did so, a soft Scots voice thanked him for supporting Stuart. It was my father, on leave from sea. Arthur Ballard and my father enjoyed a long evening in the Cracke.

John and the band also had something to celebrate. They had successfully played their way through two auditions at the Empire Theatre for the *Carroll Levis TV Star Search* talent show. The television series was fabulously popular, the equivalent of today's *Stars in Your Eyes,* so it was a huge status thing, a grand accomplishment. Johnny and the Moondogs had won a place in the finals at the Hippodrome Theatre in Manchester. The result of the talent search was based on audience applause – at the end of the evening. The groups did their turn and then returned at the end to play a short selection to remind the audience of their performance. The final applause was the vote that counted.

Sadly, John and the others could not afford to stay overnight in Manchester and left for Liverpool before the crucial moment. John complained to Stuart about the unfairness of it all, but Stuart thought they had done very well; and the girls, the judies, liked rock groups. This was a tempting bonus available to rock and rollers. Cynthia says that the official offer to Stuart to join the Moondogs was made by John in Gambier Terrace. She was there. She said that the two boys were desperate to be able to communicate on all levels. We also know that the Moondogs wanted a bass guitarist or, rather, a bass guitar and someone to hold it. Stuart had his sixty-five pounds. Cynthia explained how John put the proposition to Stuart: George played the lead guitar and Paul and John were on rhythm guitars. They needed someone on bass and Stuart could do it – he would just have to learn how to play the guitar. Quickly.

Myth and legend mix about this in the library of the Beatles, and after nearly four decades of knowing and learning and researching there are still some tales in the remarkable and unique story of the Beatles that I honestly could only spin a coin on. Paul McCartney's version of Stuart becoming a Beatle is different. When I talked to him during early research for this book he was certain that Stuart's joining up was first suggested in the Casbah. He said he saw them, quite clearly, all sitting around in what he called 'Mrs Best's place'. He thought it was a Friday. Nobody wanted to play bass, it was the instrument, the short straw, you got landed with. All the happening people were guitarists, bass players were just background people. Yet, he said, the group recognized that most bands did have one and they should too. Paul recalled John persuading Stuart to turn his financial windfall into a bass guitar. John, Paul said, told Stuart, 'Get a bass, man, because then you could be in the band. And it's not that hard, bass, you don't have to know lots of chords and stuff.' Whatever version you like – and there are many others – the two friends, Stuart and John, went off to Frank Hessy's music shop. In the window were Hofner President guitars, and by then the only question for them was blonde or brunette. John asked the question. The Hofner came in dark or blonde wood. Both boys liked blondes, and John's rhythm guitar was in light wood. The deal was done – Stuart was a member of Johnny and the Moondogs. So was the Blonde. There was one snag. Stuart did not like the group's name, the echo of groups of the day like Cliff Richard and the Shadows, Johnny and the Pirates.

Stuart had an idea. What about the Beetles?

He was a huge fan of Marlon Brando, regarding him as cinema's primitive modern male. He had seen *On the Waterfront* many times, and all the boys adored *Viva Zapata*, but his favourite Brando film was *The Wild One*, which was first screened in Britain in cinema clubs and featured a leather-clad, white T-shirted Brando as leader of a motorbike gang of fierce-looking characters. They ran with a group of biker chicks, a female group known as the Beetles. Stuart's suggestion that the band become the Beetles was accepted. John, being John and wanting to assert himself, be part of the act, later changed the spelling. For him, it was a marker and so important. He loved and admired Stuart, but John wanted not just the last word but the last letter. There wouldn't have been that group if Stuart and John had not connected. However you spell it, this was

27th March 60.
Flat 3 Hillary
Mansions
Gambier Terrace.
Liverpool.

Dear Sir, As it is your policy to present
entertainment to the habitues of your
establishment, I would like to draw your
attention to a band to the ~~Star~~ "Beatals"
This is a promising group of young
musicians who play ~~all~~ music for all
tastes, preferably rock and roll. They
have won many competitions, including Carroll Levis and auditions for
A.T.V. Unfortunately pedagogical
activities have ~~forced~~ hindered them ~~from~~ devoting
~~full~~ themselves full time to the world of
entertainment.
~~I hope you find time~~ If necessary the
~~group will give you an~~ group is prepared
for an audition, I hope you will be able
to engage them.
Yours sincerely
Stu Sutcliffe (Manager).

the moment the Beatles of yesterday, today, and tomorrow were born.

Stuart was eager to launch the group, now being spelled as the Beatals, to show-business acclaim and made a stuttering start. I have the draft of a letter he wrote soliciting engagements: 'Dear Sir, As it is your policy to present entertainment to the habitues of your establishment, I would like to draw your attention to a band, to the "Beatals". This is a promising group of young musicians who play all [sic] music for all tastes, preferably rock and roll . . .' It is signed 'Stu Sutcliffe (Manager)'. He was full of it, but first my Beatle brother still had to learn how to play his impressive but intimidating guitar; it was almost as tall as he was. John asked Dave May of the Silhouettes, who had been mooted for the bass guitarist spot, to teach Stuart a few chords, and David did his best to instruct his pupil in the chords and cadences of Eddie Cochran's 'C'mon Everybody' (you could do it on the bass mastering just three notes) and 'Summertime Blues'. John also instructed George to help teach Stuart. Progress was painfully slow as Stuart's fingers blistered and bled on the taut strings. Stuart, as ever, wanted to be perfect instantly, so there was never going to be time for the skin to naturally harden to protect itself. He also had final exams to worry about and his leading role as Fairy Snow in the college Christmas pantomime. He was better at panto than bass guitar. Stuart's tutors became concerned that damaging his hands could be detrimental to his art work. My mother was dismayed the first time she saw him with the guitar. She suspected, her intuition again, that it was a get-rich-quick scheme that would go horribly wrong. But Gambier Terrace became familiar with the musical sounds of Stuart, John, Paul, and George. It was January 1960, the beginning of a decade that would rock the world and not just Liverpool 8.

Some of Stuart's friends felt that he was wasting his time in the band. Bill Harry, despite his enthusiasm for the Quarrymen, was dismayed when Stuart told him that he was joining the band. He said he felt furious inside, disappointed. Stuart should have stayed exclusively with art. Rock and roll – it wasn't his métier. But Bill also understood that it was an escape for Stuart from his inner self, a joy and fun. Stuart was not afraid to examine and search; his letters and notes revealed much exploration of his inner self. He was always challenging me to seek other meanings and explanations for things, but with me it was always fun. I was 'the kid', and although he wanted to improve me he took a lighter tone and tried to make a giggle out of it. He was there, in his view, for me to have fun with, to enjoy being with. He was harsher with himself.

All these years later I can now see that he had some fear of failure, of disappointing, of letting down. I think too much was expected of him by himself and by us. It all seemed so easy for him. In time, of course, it all unravelled. What I do understand now is that he needed to elevate rock and roll to an art form to make it make more sense to him. Paul and George's mockery of his musical talents struck at the heart of his justification to himself. The artist in John wanted this justification also. And, of course, they both also wanted the fun. We must never forget the stimulation of applause.

For there were all the judies too. Mike Kenny and Rod Murray saw less of Stuart after he joined the band, as he was always off with John. One night Mike passed out drunk in Stuart's room. Next morning John's head appeared over the end of his divan in the corner and he demanded, 'Who the hell's this on the floor?' Stuart gave an amazed Mike a lecture about crashing out uninvited on someone else's floor. Stuart, when there were too many sleeping in his room, would sometimes come home, which was three miles away. He would also stay with us when John and Cynthia wanted some privacy. He wouldn't call it that obviously, he wouldn't say, 'I'm coming home, Mother, because I'm letting Cynthia and John have my bed.' My mother couldn't have cared less what the reason was, for she was always delighted to have Stuart home. I was too. I'd developed my hairdressing skills and Stuart wanted his hair to look a certain way; I could oblige by putting in rollers and back-brushing his hair a bit, which is what you do if you want your hair put back and sticking out at right angles to your ears.

When I first went to see Stuart play with the others at that off-duty strip club it was all really beginning. I was innocent and did not realise what a rough house it was; there were lots of people smoking marijuana, although at the time I would not have known that. Later, Stuart made sure I went to venues that did not have the Black Marias, the police vans, and Alsatian dogs waiting outside for trouble to start, but I saw it all anyway. It was hard to avoid; there was always warfare at some places, usually gang with gang, but other people often got drawn into the mayhem. Some concert spots were notorious for the violence of the audiences, including some of the group's regular venues such as the Grosvenor Ballroom in Wallasey and the Neston Institute. It was much more civilized when I saw them on 14 May 1960 at a dance hall, Lathom Hall in Seaforth, north of the city, and they were the Silver Beatles, just an adjective away from musical immortality.

That year Stuart and Veronica Johnson went with John and Cynthia and Paul and George to the Empire to see Gene Vincent and Eddie Cochran live, which to the boys was like landing on the moon. Veronica said John was furious – what a colossal irony – when the screams of female fans drowned out his idols. He yelled, face contorted, at the girls to shut up. Also present in the audience was Allan Williams, who ran the Jacaranda coffee bar in the city. Allan thought of himself as a Mr Fixit of the music scene and he was good and had connections, including the promoter Larry Parnes, known behind his back unkindly as 'Parnes, Shillings and Pence'. Allan Williams latched on to the Silver Beatles and they were given an audition by Parnes who wanted a backing group for a nationwide tour by Billy Fury. The competition included Derry and the Seniors, Cass and the Casanovas and Gerry and the Pacemakers. The Silver Beatles had no drummer, but a good player called Johnny Hutch did them a favour and sat in with them for the audition at Allan Williams's Wyvern Social Club, which would become the Blue Angel at 108 Seel Street and a haven for what were somewhat disdained as 'arty types'. There were many afternoon auditions. Stuart had his back to Parnes and the others in the audience: hearsay argues that he didn't want to display his lack of expertise, but I think it was also part of his act to be cool. He looked it in his tight jeans, black shirt, long jacket, dark glasses and wispy beard, a Bohemian cross between a Ted and an art student; it was indeed a different look. But initially not good enough for Parnes, who passed on all the groups who played for him that day. However, the effort did pay off for the Silver Beatles: a week or so later they were offered a nine-day tour of Scotland as backing group to former carpenter Johnny Gentle, another Liverpool performer. They engaged Tommy Moore on drums. He was nearly ten years older than the others and a forklift truck driver at Garston Bottle Works. He did night shifts, was in awe of his girlfriend and played the drums like a demon. Scotland was going to shake, and the Johnny Gentle tour was to take them all further than they had ever been before, to real haggis-bashing country, to Inverness, Nairn, and along the north-east coast. Often they appeared in one room playing for teenagers while in a bigger hall the more sophisticated Scots danced to traditional music. They didn't try to compete with the Jimmy Shand-style sounds and 'Long Tall Sally' was the big favourite in their repertoire.

At home, Stuart was not that much of a favourite. My mother, who suffered from and was having trouble with asthma, was becoming more stressed by the day. She was appalled that her Stuart was, as she saw it, jeopardizing his future by taking off for her beloved Scotland and not sticking close to college. She had been dismayed that Stuart had joined a band but, being open-minded, had gone to see him play. She had told Aunt Mimi who had told John, but Stuart and the others had no idea until George saw her in the audience. It was quite a shock and at first they imagined she might be there to make trouble for them. Instead, she watched and listened and was quite impressed with them. Her fears were about fights and Stuart being hurt. This was still the Teddy boy era, when violence went along with a packet of chips on a Saturday night. The Teds did not like their judies getting sweet on the band and Stuart's aloof manner attracted much attention from the girls. They were intrigued by his 'look'; he was cool. They wanted to know more about him. He had to cope with some keen fans.

Stuart also had to deal with my mother's concerns about music versus his art work. He constantly reassured her that it was like what we now call a gap year, like going to do voluntary service overseas. He said he would have finished his exams before he went to Scotland, which he did and he passed. I have his Ministry of Education National Diploma in Design – Painting: Special Subject. It is dated the day Stuart was presented with it, 1 August 1960.

A little happier, my mother was now convinced by Stuart that it was a bit of fun, it was time out, and Stuart would knuckle down and be on his postgraduate year by the autumn. Stuart could twist my mother around all of his fingers. She argued, he cajoled, she said it was a tragedy, he said it was an opportunity. Stuart smiled and hugged my mother, and he was there when the Silver Beatles – three of them renamed for the occasion: Paul Ramon, Carl Harrison, and Stuart de Stael, after the Russian-born French painter Nicholas de Stael – took the stage before Johnny Gentle's first Scottish concert in Alloa on 20 May 1960, just ten days after their audition for Larry Parnes. Johnny Gentle's attitude did not mirror his name. He was only a couple of years older than Stuart, and bought himself a pair of two-tone shoes to fit in with his backing group, but the relationship was not a glorious one. It did not really have much of a chance. The tour was hard work and there was some bad luck. Their van crashed into a stationary Ford Popular, which left Tommy Moore concussed, and minus several front teeth and good humour. Still, he allowed himself, semi-conscious and bandaged like a mummy, to be dragged by John from his hospital bed to sit behind his drum kit only hours after the accident. He survived more on the sedatives than sympathy from the band or the Fraserburgh audience. The driving, the venues, from Alloa to Fraserburgh, Inverness to Nairn, the organization, and tempers were all pretty bad. I think Stuart survived by strength of will. He told us later that it was all a mess and that John was a constant pain, always nagging. Obviously, it was not the great opportunity they had hoped for and, being miserable, they started taking it out on each other.

Paul had a real row with Stuart. Paul told me about it when we talked: 'Generally, we got on quite well but there were moments, definitely, when it was me and Stuart head to head. Unfortunately because, you know, when someone dies you don't want to . . . I hate that, for you want to be known to say to him, "Hey Stu, look mate, c'mon, we had our arguments but you're a great guy." ' Paul never got a chance to do that, as he made clear by telling me, 'I was very lucky I made it up with John before he died. That was really lucky, important, for me; probably a bit more important for John, but for me with John and Stu, I always felt a kind of a wrench at that. I didn't like what had happened.

'I remember the gigs in Scotland and staying in the hotels and we came down to breakfast in a hotel one morning and we'd started our cornflakes and were trying to wake up and Stu wanted to smoke a ciggie and everyone was, "Oh bloody hell, Stu, do us a favour. We're having our cornflakes." I think we made him sit at the next table. The joke was that his birth sign was Cancer and he had all these ciggies – no wonder he was a Cancer! It was like half a joke but it was just a flare-up, we soon got back together.'

Paul was used to such flare-ups, as he called them. In the very, very early days of the group John was trying to keep Paul out – he sniffed a rival. It was like so much of the Beatles story: it was only chance and John in a good mood that kept them together. There were lots of heated discussions. John also thought George was too young and sidelined him. Later, when Pete Best joined he wasn't arty or intellectual but he and John got on. Nevertheless, John could stir it when he wanted to: this lot were not

always the laughing cavaliers. And most certainly not in the High-
lands.

The Silver Beatles left Scotland, more broken heart than
Braveheart. My mother had to send Stuart some money to help
them get back to Liverpool but on their return they found instant
employment, a regular weekly booking at Allan Williams's Jacaranda
coffee bar and club. It was on Mondays, the night off for Allan's
popular Royal Caribbean Steel Band. I said they would have played
for a cup of tea, but Allan was more generous: at every performance
they each earned baked beans on toast and a Coca-Cola.

The beat poet Royston Ellis was in Liverpool and visited the
Jacaranda that first night the Beatles were there, and recited some
of his poems as they played. It was part of the 'arty' scene. It was also
a new world for John, Paul, George, and Stuart. They thought they
were men of the world but Paul said they were all a little un-
comfortable about Royston's poem about a sailor called 'Break
Me in Easy, Break Me in Gently'. There was not much laughter
from those hip young boys, and then they saw the inscription in
Royston's book that said that one in every four men is homosexual.
The four of them looked at each other and at each other again. On
tour some years later, Paul told me, they met up with Royston
again and he fixed John up with a girl wrapped in polythene. Paul
said, 'I heard the story next morning, as you do, and then John
wrote the story "Polythene Pam".' But that night Royston wanted
to show the Beatles a different trick – how to get high. Cheaply.
He went back to Gambier Terrace with them and produced a Vick
inhaler that he revealed had the cardboard inside impregnated with
Benzedrine. They opened one up, ate it, and stayed awake all night
talking nonsense. Whether it was the edible Vick or the excitement,
Stuart never remembered. Vick was just the start of what they
would imbibe. And not just drugs, but early success. It would have
startling results for me and my family and for the Beatles. These
were four young, unworldly men who were about to set out on
adventures which for some of them are still going on. Unhappily,

much tragedy has punctuated the saga and changed all our lives. I can't help but wonder what if? It's a terrible trait, a bad habit, but we are all victims of it. We must all learn that you cannot change history, but happily you can always, no matter what the pressure, tell the truth and that will always rewrite it for the record. It is not a comfortable process, for you have to expose weaknesses that you'd rather keep secret.

I'm sure Tommy Moore would have liked to have stayed on the musical merry-go-round if he had known what a carnival it would become but, with a couple of pounds in his pocket, he left the Beatles shortly after their Scottish excursion. However, being a kindly man, he left his drum kit behind and a pleasant but big Teddy boy called Norman Chapman took over the sticks. The drums survived only because Norman was called up for National Service three weeks later. By then Allan Williams had adopted the Beatles and found them paid bookings at two venues that were known for attracting violent audiences who indulged in post-concert punch-ups. A safer and more intriguing arrangement was to play for a generously endowed stripper called Janice; Janice wanted classical music, Beethoven if possible, to go with her G-string antics but settled for 'Summertime' and 'It's A Long Way to Tipperary', which said much for her ability to compromise artistically. I suspect she only took her clothes off because it was essential to the parts she played. Still, it meant audiences weren't looking at how Stuart played the bass, and by now he was really getting into his role as a member of the Beatles. They were becoming more popular than Gerry and the Pacemakers and Rory Storm and the Hurricanes and even a top group led by butcher's boy Teddy Taylor who (at six feet five inches tall and weighing twenty-two stone), known as Kingsize Taylor and the Dominoes, was one of the first Merseyside groups to record and for whom Cilla Black was a featured singer. John and Paul quickly became the 'voices' of the Beatles but Stuart had his solo moment with 'Love Me Tender', the title song from Elvis's first film in 1956. The girls loved that song, and Stuart enjoyed his popularity with them: he had quite a lot of girlfriends, some startlingly beautiful.

The Jacaranda's big attraction, the Royal Caribbean Steel Band, were not at all popular with Allan Williams. Without any notice they had taken off for Germany, deserted him. As he fumed over their disloyalty they had the panache – or the cheek – to send him postcards from Hamburg telling him what an exciting place it was and how much fun and money they were getting. They suggested he go over and see for himself. Always with an eye for an opportunity, big, bushy-bearded Allan, who was 29 in 1960, decided to do just that and take some recordings of the Beatles and other groups with him. His big meeting was with Bruno Koschmider, a former circus clown who had developed a more serious, entrepreneurial side. Koschmider owned the Kaiserkeller Club but was an expansionist, a shrewd business-man who was one of the overlords of the city's club empire. He told Allan of his plans to open more clubs and he needed acts, good groups that would not cost too much. Maybe twenty pounds a week. Allan produced his tapes of the Beatles, Gerry and the Pacemakers, Cass and the Casanovas, and a few others, but the recordings had been ruined; every act sounded like Minnie Mouse. On helium.

Allan, devastated, returned to Liverpool – and more bad news. Larry Parnes had cancelled a summer season for Derry and the Seniors, another of the groups that, like the Beatles, he had been informally 'managing'. This situation introduced happenstance into the story again. In an effort to placate his disappointed group he drove them in his van to London to visit the Two I's coffee bar, which was a capital showcase for rock groups. In the audience on 24 July 1960, was Bruno Koschmider. Allan, with the help of an interpreter, arranged for Derry and the Seniors to play Koschmider's Kaiserkeller Club starting the next week; they had only just begun their contract when Allan received a request to send over more rock and roll troops. Of his unofficial 'stable' only the Beatles were available but they didn't even have a drummer, essential for the German clubs. Chance appeared again.

The complaints about Saturday-night fighting and noise at the Grosvenor Ballroom had angered residents so much that Wallasey Corporation cancelled Stuart and the others' 6 August 1960 appearance. They went off to the Casbah, where Pete Best was playing drums with the Blackjacks. Mona Best had helped her son buy an impressive drum kit with calf-hide skins, which was cashmere to the usual plastic. Pete Best, who was eighteen, was good on the drums and, the golden boy that summer, he was eagerly offered a place in the Beatles line-up. Astonishingly, they made him audition at Allan Williams's Blue Angel, but it was a one drum roll endorsement and he was stamped ready for overseas duty. His mother was delighted and helped him pack. Aunt Mimi reluctantly gave John her blessing, for they both knew his art studies were perilously close to over; he did not have the grades and had no apparent interest in making them. George Harrison's father told him to boil the water before using it in Germany. His mother baked some scones – and is seen giving him them in one of the fanciful moments in the *Backbeat* film – and it was just Paul and Stuart left. Jim McCartney gave his son a lecture on behaviour and Paul, with his student passport, had the go-ahead.

At our home there was dismay, and although Stuart was allowed to take a sabbatical from college, my mother was convinced that that was all at an end. My father was at sea, and my mother fretted about his reaction to Stuart's adventure. I think Stuart did too, for he had a lasting respect for our father, who always held on to his own code and his own secrets. Stuart was always having doubts about the Hamburg trip but then John would turn up at the house and they would be laughing and joking about it – what an impact they were going to make on the Continent. John, of course, did all the Hitler routines, strutting around the front room and shouting, 'Heil, Hitler'. Remember, they were not much more than schoolboys and they were going *abroad*. As pop stars. The giggles helped to disguise their apprehension. They would wonder how they were going to do the football pools in Germany. You never think of the Beatles as football fans but John and Stuart knew all about the score draws and the rest of the arithmetic for a big win. That they had not a clue of what to expect in Germany introduced a little bit of terror, and in turn that added to the excitement of it all.

Joyce and I don't remember Stuart's leaving. It didn't make a great deal of impact on me on that particular day. He had already moved out of the house so it wasn't as if we were seeing him regularly. Allan Williams had a green Austin van and the five of them – now and forever the Beatles – crammed into it with Allan and his wife Beryl, her brother Barry Chang, and a friend of Allan's known only and always as Lord Woodbine. On 16 August 1960 they were off, leaving from the centre of town.

I didn't wave Stuart off – my mother did, but she stood in a shop doorway so that Stuart wouldn't see her and be embarrassed. She obviously reported to us where she'd been and I said, 'Oh, I hope he didn't see you – they would have taken the mickey out of him.' She assured us that she was very discreet. No doubt she wept. Hamburg was a tremendous leap of imagination; in terms of personal experience, to go to Manchester Airport was an exciting day out. I don't even think the motorway was there then. On the other hand, we had a father who probably was in South America going up the Amazon. One way in which our mother used to keep us in touch with my father was to get the atlas out and map all the journeys; he'd send letters that were always about the sun setting over the Whatsit Mountains. They were always very descriptive. On the one hand we had this sense of world geography, and on the other, our sense of geography was limited to north Wales where we used to go for a day out when my father was home. Until the awful disaster at Paris I always used to run out into the garden to watch Concorde.

five

Film Noir

'Anything could happen to them in Hamburg.'

Cynthia Lennon

Johnny B Goode.
gone, gone, gone.
Ain't she sweet
Hallelulia
Carol
Sweet Little Sixteen
Milk Cow Blues.
Move over.
True Love
Blue Suede Shoes
Honey Don't
Lend me your Comb.
Dance in the streets
Up a lazy River
Somebody Help me
Home.
Winstons Walk
Cats Walk.
Rock-a-chicka
Bebopalula.
What'd I say
Move on down the line
I don't care (if the sun)
Whole lotta shakin

IT WAS A madcap adventure as the Beatles attempted Europe the long way round, but word from Stuart in Germany arrived very quickly. My mother had a letter, and then over that period my sister and I got letters. My mother didn't have to tell Stuart to write, because he was always very attached and he learned quite early in life that if he kept her informed then she was putty in his hands. He could more or less do or get what he wanted providing he was sure to let her know what was happening, what was going on. I know now that these letters were edited versions of events. There is one letter where he talks about how miserable Liverpool is, how narrow it is, and then there are others where he is clearly homesick. What am I doing here with a sketchbook in my pocket and my fingers sore with playing the guitar when I should be painting?

They had arrived in Hamburg via Harwich and the Hook of Holland after a rotten journey, much of it sitting atop their equipment, which included the amplifier bought, through Stuart's connivance, by the art school Students' Union. All George's mother's scones had long gone and they had driven direct with only pee breaks en route. They were hungry, tired, and hugely excited as they found their way to the Kaiserkeller Club at Number 36 Grosse Freiheit, in the St Pauli district of Hamburg of which the Reeperbahn is the main thoroughfare, a sort of Amazon through that debauched jungle of a place. It was there they met Bruno

Koschmider. They were rather unkempt but the Kaiserkeller was the opposite; they liked the look of the club and its lively and exciting atmosphere. Sadly, they discovered they were going to be appearing at Number 58, the Indra, formerly a strip club and with a tiny stage just big enough to swing a bra strap. But first, said Koschmider, they must be shown their rooms, their sleeping quarters, and that's when they were taken along the street to the cinema, the Bambi-Filmkunsttheater which ran and re-ran Hollywood Westerns. The cinema's decrepit loo was their bath-room, a couple of windowless, filthy rooms behind the screen, their bedrooms. They would hear John Wayne dialogue forever in their dreams. Stuart thought it was all mad. What were they all doing there? What was he doing there? Especially, apart from John, with young men with whom he had not established a great rapport.

That was a real downer for Stuart, for all of them. It was a real grungy hole they were living in, but they wanted to be famous pop stars and they didn't turn around and walk away. Stuart had his art but what was there for any of the others to return to? They had not settled on careers: music was what motivated them. They decided to make the best of it. Derry and the Seniors were the resident group at the Kaiserkeller and an established attraction. At the Indra, exhausted and apprehensive, the Beatles crowded the small stage and began, on the evening of 17 August 1960, what was eventually to add up to more than five hundred hours of playing in Hamburg. Many days they would be at the club for almost twelve hours. There was not enough time between sets to do much else. They would start playing in the early evening and be playing the last numbers at around 2 a.m. They would alternate every hour with Rory Storm and the Hurricanes, who had Ringo Starr on drums. Nevertheless, they were often still in the club at 4 a.m. Together, they would go for breakfast, usually cornflakes, at a seaman's mission. That was one thing that had not changed in their lifestyle.

Stuart may not have been a master of the bass at the start, but with his share of guitar hours he improved considerably. He may not have been Jimi Hendrix or as good a guitarist as he was a painter, but in early Beatles terms he cut the mustard. Of course, they all got better and without doubt this was the madcap training ground that made the Beatles. At the beginning they still played a lot of Shadows numbers, but rhythm and blues took over with favourites such as Chuck Berry's 'Roll Over, Beethoven'.

They were a set of Beau Brummels with winklepicker grey mock crocodile shoes and black shirts and pants. They alternated between mauve jackets and brown ones with half-belting at the back. The beginnings of the Beatles hairstyle had begun and was controversial – it was thick at the back, almost coming over their collars. How innocent it all seems. It wasn't. Their audiences, the sailors, prostitutes, gangsters – many from East Germany following the building of the Berlin Wall – and other flotsam from that so libertine boulevard, the Reeperbahn, reflected their new environment. I didn't go to Hamburg but from Stuart's description the Reeperbahn attracted people from all over the world. There wasn't the same nightlife in Liverpool; there were seedy joints but not the Reeperbahn, which was neon, garish glamorous, and much more international. Certainly, the foreign languages made everything sound racier. Stuart wrote home about the transvestites, and how they were being pursued by some gorgeous woman and someone had to whisper in their ear that it wasn't a woman. But there was self-censorship. He didn't tell us they were known as the Peedles, which is a German vulgarity for the penis. Mind you, I don't suppose any of his family would have thanked him for that intelligence.

Stuart would sanitise everything he wrote back to us. He didn't write and say, 'we're in the dirtiest, dingiest, grottiest, most horrible place possible', in case our mother was on the first boat. He was much more frank in his letters to his friend Ken Horton, all of which I have. In one he is really questioning himself: what was he doing there? Others are more surreal, a reaction probably to the exhaustion and the pills they were all taking; part of the rationale

77

for the uppers and downers was because they played for about God knows how many hours of the day and night, every day. In one letter to Ken, Stuart wrote:

> I haven't wished you well. I still haven't but it really doesn't matter, as you are probably still as hypochondriacal as ever. We had an attack of gout, cancer, TB, polio, tonsillitis etc., in the middle of which I had my hair cut off. I wonder if you will ever get this letter as I have a tendency to forget so I had better remember now to ask you to give my regards to your friends Diana, Chris and Ronnie and any other . . . I'll be here till after Chrimbo so pull one for me. I'm not asleep yet so don't stop reading in case I think of something else to tell you.
>
> Have I told you that I sleep in a cinema? If not, write and tell me and I will be very pleased to write giving you full details by the next post. I won't need a stamped-addressed envelope until I have finished. The time is 5.20 a.m. and I am worn out. My new jacket is pretty good thank you, I'm glad you like the suede around the collar and the half-belt at the back. Yes I do think I rather looked like Frankenstein (Dr) what else is there? I'll probably be home after Christmas meanwhile rocking in Hamburg to 30-year-old-teddy-boys and 15-year-old-teddy-girls, I don't like the repetition but it'll have to do. I keep thinking that I should have spent 'haf'. I can't really get talking to the German girls because I've still got a guilty conscience about the war. I can't believe I'm not in college. Anyway as I said before we're having quite a hectic time here but Liverpool is better and I'm dying to get back and paint. I think on the sly I must be a bit mad for packing in but I must say it is quite an experience living in the mad way we do.

Mad? Well, sex, drugs, and rock and roll were indeed readily available. It has entered my mind over the years that there might have been more drug use than any of them owned up to. I don't think it would have been hard drugs. They always laughed it off as just purple hearts, uppers and downers, diet pills and brown bombers. Things to keep them awake through the night and sharp on stage. We know that much later they were all involved in drugs.

But then it was all presented in a harmless way, that a friend would go round to the chemist shop and get them the pills to keep them going. It was presented as a charming little story, like someone helping out by getting them medicine for a bad cold.

Charming is not a word I associate with Stuart in Hamburg, and not just because of his tragedy. When I reflect on it, there does seem to have been something rancid about the times and the place and the relationships between them all. Interestingly, in the book Pete Best wrote in 1985, he says he actually had a good relationship with John; his reportage of when they mugged a sailor rang so true. It was typical of John's tricks. Pete said that there were always girls, plenty of sex but not so much cash. In the audience one night was a drunk sailor who was throwing cash around. They talked about robbing him and Pete said he and John loved the idea; the others were not so keen. Finally, it was left to the two of them to take on the sailor. Pete said John hit him with a 'mean punch' and he fell to his knees. One version suggests John feared he had killed the sailor with this vicious punch.

But the sailor was not a pushover: he had been in rough and tumbles before. There was a vicious fight and Pete grabbed the sailor's wallet, but just as they were about to take off, the sailor produced a gun. They didn't know it only shot gas cartridges but, still in unison, ran at him, charging with their heads down. Gas cartridges exploded over their heads and they took off with the sailor's money. He fired cartridges after them but was too knocked about to chase them.

Pete and John would always be the first to come forward at any sign of trouble. It was only when Pete got closely involved with one particular woman in Hamburg that he started to be less involved socially with others. They all had girlfriends back in Liverpool but they were having a good time, with girls available around the clock. The girls were often a little older than they were; George was still just seventeen and the others made fun of him when they went to over-eighteen clubs, but he always went in with them. That is what it was like in Liverpool as well. Whether they had a steady girl or not there would be other girls; they were quite hot-blooded. John was the most adventurous and Pete Best reported in his book: 'John didn't like his sex to be too conventional and would regale us with details of his experiments: "I tried position sixty-eight with her standing on her head in a corner." There was no reason to disbelieve him, he was always honest about his sexual activities. "The more the merrier" he would laugh if he had been able to go to bed with two or three girls at one time. Even so, John would proudly find energy enough to masturbate as well, never trying to keep it a secret.' Cynthia has confirmed to me that John enjoyed masturbation, which gives even more veracity to Pete Best who I have always found a most honest man.

It seems the young men's appetite for sex was met by the equally hungry German music fans. Assignations were usually arranged before the beer break, and often by a glance during the first song. If living wasn't easy, the sex was; in those days maybe fame had no price, for even the professionals provided services gratis. They would go the club to see the boys play and send them drinks: whatever the group might want sexually was available later. They would all go around together, tour the sex shops, and in the windows of the Herberstrasse, the street of vice controlled by the police, often see their friends from the night before displaying their wares. Pete Best said that even the waiters would tell them the likes and dislikes, the perversions and peccadilloes, of particular girls. It wasn't just sex that was readily available – it could be customized, made to measure.

Stuart sent a letter home to Joyce and me saying, 'As far as girls go there are many but none of us can be bothered.' He was more honest in another letter: 'Recently I've become very popular both with girls and homosexuals, who tell me I'm the sweetest, most beautiful boy. Imagine it, me, the one who had such a complex because I was small and thought I was ugly. It appears that people refer to me as the James Dean of Hamburg. I'm quite flattered.

Don't imagine I am keeping the company of homosexuals. There are a few here, but all harmless and very young. They are quite happy just to sit and look. When in Liverpool I would never have dreamt I could possibly speak to one without shuddering. As it is, I find the one or two I speak to more interesting and entertaining than any others.'

His letters to Joyce and me were a little bit more informative than those to my mother, who he constantly assured about his health and his eating habits. To us, it was more gossipy and talking about what other bands were there and recordings that were available there that hadn't come to England. Of course, he used to send me Elvis Presley recordings, anything he thought would 'put me one up on the other girls'. I received Elvis's 'Wooden Heart', still in German, long before it was released in Britain. He sent me Everly Brothers records and told me that Gerry and the Pacemakers and Ringo Starr were there with Rory Storm and the Hurricanes. More interestingly to me at the time was the Ivy Benson Band, and he told me about a girl singer, Beryl Marsden, who he thought was sensational. Those were the reports I would get, and he would also make comments about my letters to him and my poor spelling. He caught me out, for he knew I substituted words I could spell rather than others that would have been closer to what I was trying to say. He was pointing out that the bad spelling was an inhibition I needed to correct; he remained very parental to me and pitched to what he thought my interests were, or should be. For example when he saw Nureyev dance – I was an absolute ballet freak – he knew that would utterly thrill me.

Away from the letters, he was playing rock and roll and enjoying the local judies. As the Beatles became more popular they had to all but fight off the girls. They had their regular 'groupies' by this time and it was an intriguing mix of fans, girls around their own age, and the more worldly professional ladies who were, maybe surprisingly, also extremely turned on by rock and roll and applause and those fresh-faced English boys. Stuart was caught in the middle of it, between two worlds; he must have felt like Jekyll and Hyde, two such different men in such a slight body, rather than Frankenstein. And which one was playing in the Beatles?

The happenings in Hamburg secured the relationship between John and Stuart. Even when Stuart stayed on in Germany and the Beatles returned to Liverpool, John and he frequently wrote lengthy, sometimes twelve-page letters to each other. Letters that have disappeared. I have known in my heart for many years that Stuart and John had a sexual relationship but to protect my mother and, out of an old fashioned sense of propriety, I kept my counsel about it although everything I knew, personally and professionally, pointed towards it. And, with hindsight, it was a lovely happening: two lost boys who needed and found each other. There have been hints published in the host of Beatles books about what happened sexually between John and Stuart. I want to set out what I believe did go on. First, to take a most recent example of the stories. In Geoffrey Giuliano's book *Lennon in America*, published in 2000, he writes that during that first trip abroad, when the Beatles were still unattached (at least in Hamburg), Paul, George, and Pete went for a day out boating with some local girls. John and Stuart went on a pub crawl along the Reeperbahn. They got thoroughly drunk and all their troubles poured out; what a shitty place it was and what were they, two artists, doing there? The drink brought out the dejection in them. When they returned to the stark room they shared, with its one bare light bulb, Giuliano conjures this scenario: 'Stu was sitting on the top bunk, while John rolled into the bottom. After a few minutes Lennon wordlessly climbed up to join Stu. What began as mutual consolation turned quietly sexual when Stu went down on him.'

Stuart performed oral sex on John Lennon? I would have thought it was the other way round. But no, if Stuart was more parental and more grown up in John's eyes, it may have happened that way. It's all inferred, even two boys in two bunks fucking girls, which was a scene in *Backbeat*, is highly incestuous. Everybody's naked, everybody's turned on. It's all very well saying they all lived in the same room, but those boys were communicating with one another, weren't they?

And with everything new and foreign that Hamburg represented. Never before had they met transvestites or transsexuals nor been importuned by them; never befriended homosexuals before; not played for eight to ten hours a night; never had free supplies of pills, booze, sex. And let's not forget how arousing and exciting live music and applause can be. All these experiences would have expanded their horizons and maybe made them feel, even for a moment, that everything was possible, everything acceptable. If you add to this potent mix the emotional intimacy and intensity of Stuart and John's personal relationship then nothing they may have done or said to or with one another would surprise or dismay me.

Geoffrey Giuliano says Derek Taylor, the veteran public relations man for the Beatles, told him in 1983 about this sexual encounter between John and Stuart. He says Taylor was, in turn, told it by Lennon during 'an intense acid trip' in 1968. Stuart would fit the pretty boy image. And, given that they all lived in such close proximity in Hamburg and had this amazingly wild and decadent life, it is very possible. It may not have been a conscious act. I don't even think for a moment that John was a homosexual, and it would not have mattered if he was. He had these little forays out, but I think he just sexualized his relationships when he was out of control. Stuart wasn't homosexual either. Not predominantly so. You just need to look at his exploration, his artistic expression as a painter and as a stylist – and his philosophical position about boundary crossing. John, of course, was immensely charismatic and strong and loved and trusted Stuart. Perhaps Stuart felt safe for them to explore that side of themselves. They had lived together in Liverpool but this was different, they were in a city where everything was possible. They were new to pills, new to this. They clearly had a very emotionally intimate relationship. Anything could have happened. This relationship was founded on much more powerful dynamics, a very intense relationship that involved part of the experimental, exploring, out of their brain stuff. It may have happened many, many times or only occasionally, when they needed the comfort of each other in that way.

I've wondered many times over the years if that's what some of the antagonism between Stuart and Paul might have been about, whether Paul suspected something. None of us directly connected to the Beatles have publicly acknowledged that John had less than conventional sexual attachments. We all thought that to ignore such things would go down better with the world, forgetting that to deny these parts of John – and John had been open to others about himself – would be to deny another level of complexity to John's personality. Therein lies the rub. John is the most loved and revered Beatle and perhaps this has something to do with his humanity and frailty and his struggle to understand himself and others.

The origins of male homosexuality are supposed to be tied up with the relationship between boys and their fathers. Or the failure of that relationship in some way, or the boys picking up some ambivalence in their fathers and all sorts of other messages. I am not convinced about such theories, but let's characterize John as a boy looking for a father's love. What other characteristics does a father have that his son would be delighted to receive from him? I know it's a big leap because Stuart didn't take him to football – although they did the pools – or anything else, but if you think about the way in which Stuart would listen to him, would try and help him make sense of what he was thinking. That's paying attention. That's developing trust. John did not have to be the big tough lout with Stuart, not all the time anyway. He could expose his sensitivity and vulnerability and trusted Stuart not to exploit this. Stuart was in touch with these qualities in himself but he did not feel the same sense of abandonment. That way he was able to provide a safety net for John. For Stuart had enjoyed our father's nurturing care and interest almost full-time until he was seven years old, when father went to sea.

But our father, even *in absentia*, was always present, if you take my meaning; he was our father whether he was at home or away. So, all of us enjoyed important early development years with him. He taught us things like cooking and made children-sized garden furniture for us to use. He was there. John had no middle-ground growing up, but his sense for the need of it, to integrate the extremes of his character, drove his life. Think of 'Make Love, Not War'. With Yoko Ono that became a world mantra, but for John it was just another way of trying to make the outer reaches of his personality meet each other. That's why John was so special. John Lennon was ahead of his time – he was seeking the Third Way. This is an essential part of the story of Stuart and John and the Beatles. John understood his own complex personality and tried to do something about it while others close to him tried to disguise it; that was a terrible, terrible mistake.

Violence in men is often associated with sexual ambivalence, and from the beginning all John's behaviour was over the top. As an analyst, and based on the material that has been available in recent years I believe John's excessive personality bordered on obsessive-compulsive disorder, which is a clinical problem. It can manifest itself in many ways: people washing their hands again and again; terrible fears of infection, of germs, like Howard Hughes. It can be trivial things like checking and checking and checking again if you have locked the front door. Over time, of course, it disrupts the life of the person suffering from it and the lives of all those around them. John's problem was overt, he was always going over the top with what he did. But I think that also disguised other scars on his personality, inner sufferings, that he could never heal. I never dealt with him as a patient so I cannot and would not want to make a definite diagnosis, but the evidence is abundant. Pete Best said that in Hamburg, John 'set the breakneck pace'. With John, everything was excessive. If there was a fight, it would be a violent fight. There was a point where he had no boundaries and no limits, as if they were not central to his personality. The infrastructure wasn't there and I think that's clear throughout his life; it was evident well before he or the Beatles were anything like famous. The core of his personality wasn't developed enough.

Stuart's tutor in the sculpture class at art school, Philip Hartas, described John to me as a guy like a car without brakes – a fabulous metaphor. If it's a nice, flat road it won't travel far – but face it down a hill . . . That runs through all John's profligacy: too much drugs, every drug that's ever been thought of in the world, and his willingness to have sex with Stuart. It's quite possible that whether he was blind drunk or drugged he would cross those boundaries without there being any deliberate homosexual intent.

After John's son Julian was born, John went on holiday to Spain with Brian. It is now widely believed that they had homosexual sex on one occasion during that trip. John talked of it as him being kind to Brian. But it was not just a one-night stand in Spain and he attended gay parties in England with Brian and other men I know. There was lots of talk in Liverpool about John, for in those days the suggestion of such peccadilloes was scandalous and the act itself still illegal.

John Lennon was a man who could have been seriously helped through good, sound, orthodox intervention. Instead, he tried a myriad of different therapies, everything, it seemed, except the traditional ones. It was the catch-22 of his condition – he always went to extremes, in this case undergoing primal scream therapy when that was the last thing he needed. I am trying to explain what has for so long appeared inexplicable about what happened between my brother and my family and the Beatles. It is not about redefining John's sexuality. He was clearly predominantly hetero-sexual; that was obviously his first choice but with his kind of personality, whatever other alternatives were available whether it be drugs, drink, or sex, there would be a moment in time when he wouldn't know his controls had gone.

The controls, those brakes, wouldn't have gone on like they do with most people; he wouldn't have heard that little voice of reason. It doesn't surprise me at all that John experimented and explored everything. I am really and sincerely not intent on causing a fuss by writing this: I do so because I believe it is an essential part of the big picture. I suggest further evidence would be how compulsive he was about Yoko Ono, how he could so easily walk away from Cynthia and his son Julian, how he could later just walk away from Yoko, and in turn from his girlfriend May Pang without even considering if she could pay the rent in their shared apartment in Manhattan, or how she could get her life back after his disruption of it.

This isn't because he was an evil man; it was a failure to take responsibility for his own behaviour and actions, which is consistent with an obsessive-compulsive disorder. Intelligently, Philip Hartas also saw John as someone who was living off the top of his head. Of course, the Beatles' success provided the avenue for him to lavishly do that with utter abandon because there were no limits, he could have anything he wanted. He was a victim of his celebrity, a fool of fortune. Yet, the man was there before the Beatle.

Clearly, there were forced moments in the Beatles' camaraderie. John was the instigator of many schemes, and although they might not want to join in they mostly did, for in the early days they had no option but to look on themselves as a team. There was strength in the Musketeer philosophy of all for one and one for all. But early events in Hamburg rattled even that confidence. The Beatles had played the Indra for a month when Bruno Koschmider detached Stuart from the rest of the group and sent him to play with the bigger and more popular band at the Kaiserkeller, his major venue. He was not a back-slapping, eager-to-please man but he tried at all times to keep his groups as happy as possible for the lowest possible cost. He was a cold fish but a wily businessman: if the boys were happy they were more likely to make the audiences the same way and the drinks would flow even more.

Bruno was thinking serious business when he decided to put on a second group instead of the jukebox in the interval, and the cheapest way was to split the Seniors in two. The first unit now comprised Derry Wilkie on vocals plus two guitars and drums; the second was made up of Seniors' Howie Casey on sax, Stan Foster on piano, Stuart on bass, and a German gentleman on drums. Howie Casey told me about this first break-up of the Beatles: 'All we could do with Stu was to play twelve-bar blues. He couldn't venture out of that and I noticed more than ever how self-critical he was about his music all the time. In those early days none of us were exactly brilliant musicians. He used to sketch around the club, drawing patrons and members of the group. He had a good image, quiet, mean, and moody, but with us he was one of the boys. He wasn't at all stand-offish, and he had a nice sense of humour. The Beatles did their nut because Stu was playing with us.' Stuart's musical talents must have measurably improved to make them so upset at losing him to another band.

Stuart was still obliged to return in the wee hours of every morning to his horrid room behind the cinema screen. His brain in overdrive, he would find it difficult to sleep and would write letters and thank heaven for that. The letters are some of the memories of him we can touch and look at and feel. He'd been roughing it in Liverpool, of course, but this was something else: sordid surroundings, punishing hours, a mercurial boss, no mother popping in with food and clean laundry. In one line of a letter to Susan Williams he spills out some of the heartache: 'Hamburg has little quality, except the kind you would find in an analysis of a test tube of sewer water. It's nothing but a vast amoral jungle.'

For a woman living above the Indra club it was not so much a question of morality. Or amorality. It was noise. She could live with the strippers but not the noise of the resident rock and roll band. Her complaints to the police were strong enough to force Bruno Koschmider to shut the Indra and reunite the Beatles at the Kaiserkeller. Derry and the Seniors had been replaced by Rory

Storm and the Hurricanes (Ringo on drums), with whom the Beatles would play split shifts. Before this Stuart had written to Ken Horton:

Actually I'm only writing at the moment because I can't sleep — it's about 6 a.m., and I can just about read what I am writing. I've just decided that at Christmas I pack in rocking and join the club again — you know, the old jeans and sweater gang with a pencil and sketchbook. I've decided that if I get back I might yet be able to make something of myself.

I've forgiven you by now so I'll be matey and say sorry for the beginning. but who cares, I don't give a damn about anything (anymore). I wonder whether I ever did though. I'm a bit frightened at the prospect of returning. there'll be so many new faces, and people doing exciting things. I've got indigestion and my throat is burning like God knows what and smoking like a chimney — about 40 a day. my girl-friend in Liverpool — the one I write to — hasn't written for two weeks. that last letter she sent she told me about some girl who was going round carrying my child (not yet born). How's that for a laugh, it's the first I'd heard I was a father-to-be.

If I had great musical sense I could place tin cans round the room, all different sizes and as the rain fell in I could arrange it so that I'd composed a little tune, but I'm more content to just listen to the dull thuds and thwacks the raindrops make as they hit floor and bed.

When I come home at Christmas it'll be for good, also without guitar probably — I'll sell it if I can. Mind you, except for you (I think) I'll be absolutely friendless when I do return but who cares, I never really had any friends anyway.

Where Stuart got the idea about fatherhood is a mystery. The girls around at the time, Veronica Johnson and Susan Williams, all thought it highly improbable. It might well have been Stuart making mischief, for Veronica recalled a similar story Stuart told her months earlier about another member of the group getting a girl pregnant. That, indeed, was a far more complex saga not *directly* involving the Beatles, and for that reason and to protect people I will not delve into it here. At that time the gossip from home was welcomed by Stuart and he and the others would discuss and dissect it, just as Stuart and John had chatted for hours in the Cracke pub about the problems with college, girls and the tutors. In Hamburg they had other concerns.

At the Kaiserkeller, they had to do more than stand around on a small stage – they had to fill a big one. On a visit, Allan Williams shouted at them to 'Make a show!' and the German fans took it up with cries of 'Mach schau!' if enthusiasm was fading. It became the legendary Beatles refrain, 'Let's Go'. The fans fuelled the perform-ances, especially John's, by sending crates of beer up to the stage. The beer and the pills – Pete Best was never tempted by the uppers and downers – made for a lively effect on stage. The longer the night, the wilder the antics. There's one photograph of Stuart with a Cheshire cat grin watching John almost doing the splits on stage. Suddenly, Stuart was enjoying the rock and roll life and when their contract was extended until the end of the year he wrote to Susan Williams in a letter I have:

> I believe we are going to Berlin after Christmas, but don't mention this to Cynthia yet in case John hasn't told her, because in a letter he received today she says she can't wait for Xmas and him. I had a burst of enthusiasm and bought a lot of paper and charcoal etc., but after about a dozen poor drawings, I'm afraid my enthusiasm waned a little. I know full well the only thing is to keep at it. I have fully resigned myself to about a year away from art and expect to pay the consequences, but in due course this will become another barrier to overcome and I usually strive better under the face of adversity. I've just had to buy another amplifier for my guitar which is costing £120. I'm paying it weekly at £7 but unfortunately my boss won't sign the HP papers – but I have the amplifier! John has just come in and we talked a little. I definitely want to get painting again. I see so many things in my mind, things that only need [to be] made concrete and they would

be good but I can't transpose them yet, I must wait, after all I came
away with the full intention of forgetting painting for a few months,
in order that I would forget my tricks and then return with an open
mind. One thing for sure about since I've been here, I hate brutality,
there is so much in this area.

There was also tension at home for our mother. She told Stuart
of the repercussions from the upheaval at the Gambier Terrace flat;
the rental agents had sued Rod Murray for damage to the property.
With Stuart and John abroad, Rod contacted my mother, with
whom he always had a wonderful relationship. It caused quite an
upset between Stuart and Rod, who had been Stuart's best friend
from the day he started at art school. Rod rightly felt dumped with
the rent and their things, all their belongings, that were going to get
thrown out unless we picked them up. Rod told us to get there
before he was finally thrown out and the doors locked up. I went
with my mother and we retrieved as much as we could, including
some items of John's such as his *How to Draw Horses* book. Later,
she gave the book and other items back to John. But that was after
Stuart had gone. Meanwhile, there were letters going backwards
and forwards between Rod and Stuart and then my mother got
quite a haughty reply from Stuart. And he could be quite haughty
sometimes – he wasn't always peace and joy. It was all about how
he didn't feel he owed Rod anything. He listed reasons why he
didn't think he did. At the time I believed my brother, but with
hindsight I think that was a bit irresponsible and I don't think it was
very kind. He thought he could offload the responsibility because
he had John living there, and Cynthia, Paul, and George now and
again. Despite all of that Rod has retained his marvellous memories
of a fabulous friendship with Stuart, so it didn't invade.

After the Rod Murray debacle was resolved, for me, back in
Liverpool, it was all blue skies. I was growing up and becoming a
real rock and roll fan. I ran to the postman most days, always
expecting a letter from Stuart. And hoping for a present of a record

that was not in the Liverpool music shops. One wet Saturday morning in October I was up later than usual and there was an envelope waiting for me at the breakfast table. My mother was anxious to know the contents but would never have thought of opening Stuart's letter or even hurrying me up. There was procedure, the correct way of doing things. I tore the letter open:

> We have improved a thousandfold since our arrival and Allan Williams, who is here at the moment, tells us that there is no band in Liverpool to touch us. Rory Storm is on the stage doing his act . . . the Hurricanes have just done 'Shakin' All Over', another number which we have made popular. Our biggest numbers being 'What'd I Say', 'Tutti Frutti', 'Long Tall Sally', 'Lucille', 'Sweet Little 16', 'Johnny B. Goode', 'Three Steps to Heaven' and quite a few more. All the singers have lost their voices at one time or another except Paul. At the moment George is out of action, but hopes to be singing again soon.
>
> While writing, my mind is filled with the letters I will shortly have to write, one to my mother and one to my father. This will be the difficult one, particularly as I have made no contact with him for over a year, and in view of my, what must seem to him, imbecile choice of coming to Hamburg. Anyway I will cross those bridges when I come to them.
>
> Of the love I send, give a fair proportion to Joyce and my mother, and if my father is home, him too.

The next Saturday, as if by rote, there was another letter. It was addressed to me and Joyce and enclosed photographs an unnamed girl had taken of him. He was hoping for more photographic sessions and better results and wrote with Cupid on his shoulder:

> I can imagine she'll have a difficult job doing something with them as the weather at the time was appalling. It was raining, believe it or not (drizzle), and I wasn't looking so good with pimples and my hair is a mess. But I'm quite pleased with these, as the lads say, "typical Dean poses". The dual photo is excellent and the texture just like a painting.

Next Monday they have invited me to dine with them in a Chinese restaurant. Tomorrow the boy [Klaus Voormann, an art student] *is going home to Berlin to see his parents so I won't see them for a few days. I'm quite pleased with them because everyone else likes them (in the band) and I'm pleased with my 'find'. I've got a bit of new stuff here, new sports jacket, suit, suede-type jacket off John which I'm wearing on the photos – I'll have this cleaned and it'll be fab. I've just remembered that my mum thinks that I'm still growing my beard. Well, as you can see on the photos, I'm not, in fact I shaved quite a few weeks ago.*

He had met Astrid Kirchherr. She was two years older than Stuart and all things blonde and bright and beautiful. Their encounter changed everything. We can have no control over events or the people we encounter and what we see as an escape route. If Stuart's new life began when he bought that bass guitar, it was turning somersaults when he met Astrid. Sitting in my kitchen chair in Liverpool, playing my German version of 'Wooden Heart', reading Stuart's letters, I could never have anticipated what was going to happen. I am sure for others it was not on the level of a Greek tragedy, but for our family it was to be just as tumultuous and a drama that is still going on.

six

The Glass Slipper

'He was a major attraction because of the James Dean thing, the dark, moody thing. I think a lot of people liked that.'

Paul McCartney on Stuart in Hamburg

you are the best photographer
in the world.
And you look lovely when
you take them.

ASTRID. OUR FAMILY could never have anticipated the impact she was to make on us all. When we read Stuart's letters we had images of such an exotic creature, and my besotted brother had presented her much as she was. Even through his fond, loving gaze he had managed to convey a not too exaggerated picture of her. She arrived at our house like a Cinderella. I was a tiny teenager. This was some intimidating, blonde-haired foreign woman who was in love with my brother. I was in awe. She was an alien to me in every sense. Her English was not very good and her smiles, displaying dazzling teeth, and shrugs during conversation when she couldn't understand what we were saying only added to the allure, the somewhat disturbing mystery of her. She had a deep voice and a throaty laugh and you could see her confidence in her gaze. That added, for me, very much to her grown-up image; it made her even more the sophisticated older woman in my brother's life.

She had her hair closely cropped, with soft sideburns curling around her ears. In Liverpool, it was back-combed hair and perms, mascara, and tight skirts and high heels. The dolly-bird look, miniskirts, and Mary Quant make-up were still a little time away. Astrid was so different and she wore little make-up. Now, she could have walked out of a Giorgio Armani store: her look was clean-cut, simplistic, and she mostly wore black. Her appearance and attitude were ahead of our, if not her, times. She cast a spell.

Stuart enjoyed his close encounters with this new and fascinating species. Of his first meetings with Astrid and her friends he said in a letter: 'Just recently I have found the most wonderful friends . . . the most beautiful trio I have ever seen. I was completely captivated by their charm. The girl thought I was the most handsome of the lot. Here was I feeling the most insipid working member of the group, being told how superior I looked – this alongside the great Romeo John Lennon and his two stalwarts Paul and George – the Casanovas of Hamburg!'

When I talked to Paul McCartney, we spent some time discussing the catalyst for the romance between Astrid Kirchherr and Stuart. Paul said to me all these years later about Stuart: 'Well, certainly he was a major attraction because of the James Dean thing, the dark, moody thing. I think a lot of people liked that. But that's a little bit surface. I think he contributed an intellectual spirit we were all happy to pick up on. Stuart was a little more "swotty" than us, he knew a little more, he was a little older than me. Stuart's artistic quest was within the group. I don't think anybody noticed that offstage, except the exis and Astrid, Klaus and Jurgen.'

When Paul talks of the 'exis' he is referring to the city's existentialist crowd who dressed in velvet and suede and leather, very much a unisex set of people who favoured black set off with white collars or ruffs at the wrists. Klaus was Klaus Voormann, a Berliner who had been going out with Astrid since 1958. Jurgen was Jurgen Vollmer his friend and a photographer. Klaus was seventeen, anxious for a career in fashion, and studying illustration at the Meister Schule, when he began dating fellow student Astrid. She was taking dress design classes. Later, Astrid's lover became a lodger with her and her widowed mother, Nielsa, at their elegant, three-storey temple to Gothic taste and antiques at 42 Eimsbutteler Strasse. Klaus had qualified as a graphic artist by the time the Beatles arrived in Hamburg, and at that time Astrid and her mother had heard all about his obsession with rock and roll. Astrid, who was twenty-two, dressed in black polo sweaters and her long legs emerged in fishnet stockings from tight leather skirts. The exi men wore trousers and that, apart from gender geography, was the only difference. They were, at first sight, a serious, humourless bunch but they would go wild to the sound of live music. Klaus liked the nightlife and after an argument with Astrid – fate, yet again – he went off in a huff and found himself walking into the Kaiserkeller. The Beatles were onstage and Klaus heard 'Roll Over, Beethoven' and John Lennon doing Hitler and Nazi jokes. The audience, to Klaus's surprise, roared for more music – and jokes. John would always oblige with a goose step and a string of expletives.

Klaus returned for another rock and roll fix, and as a passport to the Beatles took along a German record sleeve he had designed for the Ventures' song 'Walk, Don't Run'. He gave it to John who instantly handed it to Stuart, explaining to Klaus: 'He's the artist in the group.' Stuart and George and Paul were more pleasant than John, but he too came round when Klaus bought the drinks. Two evenings later Klaus returned with his friend Jurgen and with Astrid, who was reluctant to venture into such a tough area of the city but did not want to appear so. The exis trio stood out in the audience of rockers. Onstage, Stuart and the others were wearing leather jackets and their tight pants. Astrid thought the music sensational, the outfits she would have to think about. She watched Stuart but could not tell if behind his dark glasses he was looking at her. Of course, he was. They all were.

Astrid had been instantly attracted to Stuart: 'Stu looked quieter than the others. I couldn't see Stu's eyes behind those dark glasses but I knew, somehow I just knew, he was looking at me. I also knew that one day there would be something real between us.'

Stuart's image fitted perfectly with the existentialists, and when they found out he was a painter they were even more impressed by him. The James Dean tag has always been a red herring, for Stuart modelled himself on another actor: the image was originally inspired by the Polish star Zbygniew Cybulski, whom Stuart had first seen in *Ashes and Diamonds* at the art school film society. Bill

Harry ran the society and he and Stuart were taken by the style of Cybulski, the lookalike of a young Jean-Paul Belmondo, with wavy, swept-back black hair, and cool sunglasses and manner. For Stuart, Cybulski was playing him, up on the big screen. Astrid was involved in smaller images.

Astrid by then was an apprentice photographer at the studio where Jurgen was employed as a junior assistant. They both wanted to photograph the Beatles, this British rock group. Jurgen was as nervous as he was keen and told me about that first encounter: 'You went down into a cave and it was very dark – you felt there was no escape, it was just like prison. We edged our way through the crowd towards the band because it seemed the safest place to be. The rest of the customers were mostly rockers, who didn't seem to be paying much attention to the band – to them the music was just a backdrop to their talking, flirting, dancing, or fighting. In the Kaiserkeller I lived in constant fear. We saw so many brutal fights. They used to throw tables at each other, and the waiters would be hitting the drunks. But we went there literally every night out of sheer fascination with the Beatles. John looked really menacing, while Stuart wore sunglasses and was the most mysterious one. He was of course immediately interested in Astrid, for she was very striking-looking.'

Astrid's attraction worked on all of them, and they agreed to meet her for a photographic session the next day. Stuart wrote me a letter about it. Astrid had never even been in the St Pauli district of the city before that night in October 1960, but she quickly took control; here she was getting them, according to Stuart, into 'typical James Dean poses', before running films through her camera. The Beatles posed at the Dom; on a carousel and a Ferris wheel at the city funfair; by an old lorry; and outside a circus-style tent. Stuart wore a suede jacket he had bought from John for a couple of pounds and a pack of cigarettes. And these were the pictures that had arrived with my letter that Saturday morning. Pimples and all. And the first whiff of Astrid.

There is such a thing as love at first sight, and the attraction between Stuart and Astrid was instant and mutual. Paul told me: 'He was just so in love and it peeved the rest of us like mad that she hadn't fallen in love with any of us. It was something none of us had ever seen before; none of our parents had that sort of relationship. It was a wild scene to us.'

Stuart, obviously more thoughtful and heartfelt about it, was not so sure. In a troubled letter full of poetic and at times disturbing imagery, he told Ken Horton of his new love. Dated 8 November, he said he was writing from the Kaiserkeller and talked of it as being 'empty, like a huge pair of dirty wet underpants waiting for the right tool to pour its rich semen through the ugly distorted slit provided in order that man may piss away the badness from his 24 feet long coil of intestines.'

In five crammed pages he went on veering between joy at having found love – and fear it might distract him from his search for a purpose in life:

How I long for clarity and yet how I loathe these precise men, who are never satisfied until they have labelled, ranged and set aside each separate emotion, ignoring their gradations. How to make them see the world of shifting forms in which I live? Now that I begin to isolate my destiny I find it is like those plants which we can never dig up with their roots intact. I am completely alone, I never find happiness for long with a girl.

I do love a girl but I will speak little of her for my mind would overflow with tenderness. She's like a rose that has run its dark leaves over the wall to look at the sun. complexion slightly pale, eyes full of fire and now full of dew. Her hand white, beautiful and tiny – trembling. So saintly she might have walked the waves of a lake and the unshivered lake would have borne her tiny feet. I am aflame, a woman's beauty is not, as the priest says, a temptation of the devil, but may, when in her spirit, work miracles. But!!! she has a boyfriend, I'm sure she loves him and certainly he her, although no sign of affection is passed between them.

In a piss-pot sits my soul. I rainbow cupola of thought – you are my church! How can I help being bored here? The stage is so small, so unmasterly set. Should I write or not write. Better still I walk out with my tie in a beautiful knot.

1.15 a.m. I have just recovered from another visit from my strange and beautiful friends. She handed me a chocolate heart encased in silver paper and wrapped in red cellophane, oh the heartache!! Tomorrow I will buy a white rose, a young boy's thought, a sunny thought and golden one, marred only by the knowledge that I will never have the courage to give it to her. On Monday she takes more photos of me, by the river with my guitar, if it could speak your ears would burn with the heat of my message.

Time, which always spells defeat for love, treats hate more slowly – but the end in either case is the same. Hate is so much a part of the anguish that love gives that we must be so careful, we must know ourselves sufficiently well to treat each passion not as an entity but as a force related to each other. I'm beginning to dislike this letter, now the time is 4.10 a.m.

It was all emotive material, but we still did not know Asrtrid's name. Stuart's concern was clearly her relationship with Klaus but always that seemed to be a side issue with her. Her relationship with Klaus was never over, it was as if it had never begun. She was, as far as I can discover, much more mature than you would expect about it. Klaus had lived with her in the annexe flat she had at her mother's home, and soon Stuart would take over that space. That is what he wanted as he spent the time before his first full day – and solo photographic session – with Astrid by writing a letter to Susan Williams. He began with an apology for filling his previous letter with references to his new friends, and then proceeded to repeat the offence:

Sorry; but they have a profound influence on me. More so now than before, I can't explain it. it's as though they owned part of me so that when we meet, both parts meet and form the whole of me. Very weird

and ghostly. tomorrow I meet the girl, she's going to take more photos,
the first of her freelance career. I hope for her sake they are successful.
Perhaps it's my loneliness here, but I find I love her very much. Still,
after tomorrow I will know for sure as after a whole day in her
company something's bound to happen.

It did. Like the snap of your fingers. Stuart had now fallen
deeply in love with Astrid. He had enjoyed quite a lot of girlfriends,
some quite startlingly beautiful who would have tested his prowess,
so he was certainly sexually experienced. More than most, I would
think. If I bear in mind that Astrid could barely speak a word of
English and Stuart was communicating out of a German dictionary
I have to conclude that it was physical at first.

That is supported by Stuart's actions, for he was not at first
totally convinced of his conquest. Klaus was still a concern, and
Jurgen recalled to me Stuart's constant questioning: 'I remember
sitting with him at a table and giving him a detailed description of
Astrid's life. He wanted to know all about her – how long she had
been with Klaus, and the relationship between them.' Jurgen was
intrigued by his friend's reaction to Stuart's entanglement with
Astrid: 'When the romance developed, I was surprised how Klaus
took it. He seemed completely cool and there was apparently no
hard feeling.'

There were, in other areas. A rival club, the Top Ten, opened in
the Reeperbahn with Tony Sheridan and the Jets the resident act.
The Beatles were impressed, for Sheridan had a strong, as it were,
track record with recording releases and television appearances. He
was a star and the Beatles wanted to play with him, and during
breaks from the Kaiserkeller they began jamming with him at the
Top Ten. Sheridan remembered: 'We'd all met up in a striptease club
called Studio X. We were only playing there for a week or so, while
they finished decorating the Top Ten. We had to play in the break
when the ladies were taking their bras off, which is all it was in
those days. One evening the Beatles came in and just sat down and

listened to what we were doing. I remember George telling me he'd bought over a guitar like the one he'd seen me playing on the *Oh Boy!* television show. It was a rubbish guitar, really, a copy of a Fender, and by this time I'd got rid of mine and was into real guitars, Gibsons. But that's how obsessed George was with what he was doing.'

Bruno Koschmider, who I said was a strong businessman, had hard feelings. He did not enjoy the competition from the Top Ten and was infuriated by what he saw as the Beatles' disloyalty in playing there. He fired them – with a month's notice. At the same time he withdrew his protection of the seventeen-year-old George Harrison: the authorities learned of the illegal presence of a minor in a Hamburg nightclub after midnight and George, three months short of his eighteenth birthday, was deported. Stuart was rather lost by all this. He was overwhelmed by Astrid and spending every moment he could with her, but concerned about what was happening with George. Astrid was fond of George; she had mixed with all the boys during the photographic sessions and she was always around the club. Although she was with Stuart she became a Beatles mascot, a cheerleader. She was glamorous, different, and interested, and they all liked her and were jealous of Stuart. It was Astrid and Stuart who saw George off from the Hauptbahnhof, the railway station. George, not a tactile sort, unusually, astonishingly, embraced them both before cramming himself, guitar, and amplifier into a second-class carriage. And a packet of apples from Astrid's mother.

It was a rather ignominious end to George and the Beatles' first spell in Hamburg. Was it an omen, for that bad luck happened just as Stuart's dreams were soaring? He and Astrid had got engaged, exchanging rings in the German tradition, seven weeks after they had met. Stuart was nineteen years old.

The engagement did not sit well with John, for Astrid had disrupted an older, intimate bond. Now, the slightest inflection in Stuart's voice when Astrid was present would send John into a foul mood. He was easier when Stuart was on his own but when Astrid was around, John would pepper her with one-liner put-downs. Stuart was stuck in the middle of this, a severe stretch of loyalty. What is your answer to: Who do you love the most? It was a painful scenario. John became less abrasive with time and his barbs at Astrid became more like those he mauled Stuart with, rough but affectionate. It was as though John accepted that this was the way it was. Full stop. There were other problems for Stuart. After all the hours of playing he was a much improved musician, but Paul and George constantly niggled about his abilities.

More galling, it was Stuart who had conquered and won the exotic, blonde Astrid. It was an intriguing, emotional melting pot, but events outside their control took over. Without Bruno Koschmider's caretaker role, their work permits were closely screened in December 1960: they had worked illegally for three months. Events ran into each other. When Paul and Pete Best were clearing out some of their belongings there was a small fire at the Bambi-Filmkunsttheater. It involved a smoking rag and not much damage was done, but they were accused of trying to burn down the cinema. Stuart and John had already moved their clothes and things to the Top Ten. Paul and Pete were deported after spending a few hours in jail.

Later, Stuart and John were interviewed by the police. That December, Aunt Mimi remembered John arriving home in the early hours one morning. In Hunter Davies's authorized biography of the Beatles, he quotes Auntie Mimi about John's return: 'He had these awful cowboy boots on, up to his knees they were, all gold and silver. He just pushed past me and said: "Pay that taxi, Mimi." '

Stuart was freed by the police after signing a statement that he knew nothing about the fire – or the evidence, which was a charred rag. He wrote home with his news on 2 December, and I think he thought it might please our parents and help mend fences:

Surprise, surprise! We finished in Kaiserkeller last week. The police intervened because we had not work permits. Paul and Peter the drummer were deported yesterday and sent in handcuffs to the airport. Now only John and I remain. John goes home tonight, and I stay at Astrid's house till Xmas. (Her mother will feed me and keep me in cigarettes till then.) The last few days have been rather hectic, and we've not known what has been happening next. We were supposed to work in the Top Ten but the police again intervened. I haven't written sooner because I wanted to see matters settled. I don't think I've had any letters from you or some time so I assume you are rather annoyed about the whole situation. I don't know what you or my father would have done in the same situation, but I don't feel I've let you down. Anyway, till I hear from you – write to Astrid's address.

Stuart was more forthcoming in a letter to Ken Horton. It was written around 10 December and posted on 19 December, and first he told Ken about his engagement to Astrid who he described as his 'too wonderful little angel-girl'.

I have Stuart's letter to Ken and it is revealing of his mood at the time. And of his concern for little or anyone other than Astrid. This is a man in love with love, besotted:

She flew down a few weeks ago, and big bad man Stu said, I'm better than God, stay with me. Actually I'm her church and she's the bells that ring. She pulls the ropes and can she swing. it all happened about two weeks ago when she proposed photographing my wonderful face. She photographed and I proposed, and here I am living in the lap of luxury and contentment. Better than the cell I spent a night in last week.

I was innocent this time though, accused of arson – that is, setting fire to the Kino (cinema) where we sleep. I arrive at the club and am informed that the whole of Hamburg Police are looking for me. The rest of the band are already locked up, so smiling and very brave on the arm of Astrid, I proceed to give myself up. At this time I'm not aware of the charge. All my belongings, including spectacles are taken away

*and I'm led to a cell, where without food or drink I sat for six hours
on a very wooden bench. and the door shut very tight.*

*Half asleep at two in the morning I signed a confession in
Deutsch that I knew nothing about a fire and they let me go. The
next day Paul and Pete were deported and sent home by plane, John
and I were without money and no job. The police had forbidden us
to work as already we were liable to deportation for working three
months in the country illegally. The next day John went home. I stay
till January at Astrid's house. At the moment she's washing all my
muck and filth collected over the last few months. God, I love her so
much.*

*I hope you don't mind this rather factual note, but there is no
poetry to spare for writing — it's all for love. She has bought me paper
and inks and crayon and I mess about pretending to work, while she
washes etc. Her ex-boyfriend who I love very much is on the verge of
suicide — too bad.'*

In Liverpool, we had found out about the engagement at the
end of November when Stuart wrote to my mother suggesting she
might think he had found a replacement for her. My brother was
the only one of the Beatles still in Germany when he wrote from
Astrid's home on 24 December 1960:

*So here I am, Christmas Eve in a strange country — in all a strange
atmosphere — I like it. The Advent seems to be celebrated more sincerely
here than at home. Astrid tells me very few people get drunk. I had a
letter from George today. He tells me he likes the flat — 'fab'. But you
didn't seem very keen on the idea of me getting engaged. I hope you
have become used to the idea by now. Astrid has bought me a black
polo for Xmas. She's waiting to go and post this now. So bye-bye,
happy crimbo, Astrid sends her love and best wishes for Xmas to you
all at home.*

Stuart was always protective of my sister Joyce and me, but by
now we were getting out and about and going to clubs. I would

write to him about the clubs but he was always warning us to be careful. It was around this time that he told me about going to the ballet with Astrid. I was giving him gossip from the Cavern. In one letter I reported that Paul and his girlfriend Dot had split up, and so he writes back asking who dumped who? Is Dot upset or what? Was it because of Paul's womanizing? Tell me more. Can't you ask your friend Susan, because she mixed with them? I had to be careful, for that Christmas time I had gone – shock, horror (well, it was to me) – to an all-night party at Susan's. And the rest of the Beatles were there.

Susan had this horribly grotty flat in Princes Park, and in those days one had all-night parties and somehow I managed to get permission to stay. The three Beatles were there, George, Paul, and John, and dozens of other people. They didn't acknowledge me at all which, in the circumstances, was just as well.

One of the Cavern bicycles was in another room and I noticed the frequency of visitors to that other room, which included John, Paul, and George, and it took me ages to figure out what was going on, such was my innocence. Truly. I spent the hours figuring out how I was going to get home. I smoked even then because I remember, when Paul was leaving at dawn, everybody had run out of cigarettes. They were all scrounging off one another and so there was a big hoo-ha about no cigarettes. Paul then put his overcoat on, took a packet of cigarettes out of his pocket and then quickly put them back. It reminded me that Stuart had told me how careful he was. He had also told me how he and John used to borrow money from Paul with the sole purpose of not paying him back; they enjoyed winding him up.

I never went to another all-night party ever. I thought it was the seediest, grungiest event that I had ever been to in my life. Cynthia never went to them or many other parties; everybody protected her from what was going on between John and other women. The Beatles were used to being awake most of the night in Germany, the vampire hours. I reported this back to my brother, not in this sort of detail, but that I had been to this party at Susan's and that the Beatles were there.

Stuart's reply was thunderous: 'Don't you ever go near them – they are a bad lot.' I was amazed. These were his friends, weren't they?

seven

Bad Blood

'Can't you come home sooner – if we get a new bass player it will be crummy and it's no good with Paul playing bass.'

George Harrison, in a letter to Stuart

Mrs M Sutcliffe
53 Ullett Rd.
Sefton Park.
Lwerpool 17
Lancs.
England.

MIT LUFTPOST
PAR AVION

My beautiful darling. I love you.
Thank you so much for your love.
and your chocolate and lette.
I love you. your little boy. I kiss you. X

BEATLEMANIA. I WAS present at the first scent of it. Disenchanted from their abrupt removal from the Continent, John, Paul, and George at first couldn't find themselves, never mind a gig, on their separate returns to Liverpool. It was the middle of December 1960 before they all made contact and spent time hanging around their old haunts like the Casbah. Pete Best was the moving force at this time, helping to get not just the group but their equipment back together. In Germany, Paul had played the bass when Stuart was not around. This, at first, was the plan for the reunited Beatles when they played once again for a home audience. George was not happy with this plan and wrote to Stuart in Hamburg: 'Can't you or won't you come home sooner, as if we get a new bass player for the time being, it will be crummy, as he will have to learn everything, and it's no good with Paul playing the bass, that is if he had some bass and amp to play on.'

Stuart stayed with Astrid. Chas Newby, who had played the Casbah with the Blackjacks, became a temporary replacement until New Year's Eve that year for Stuart on bass. Not surprisingly, their first return date was the Casbah, on 17 December 1960. It went well – they made a good show. On Christmas Eve they brought the Grosvenor Ballroom in Wallasey alive, and three days later in north Liverpool a landmark in Beatles history was established. The all-night Hamburg sessions paid off and the town hall audience in

Hatton Hill Road, Litherland, had never seen or heard anything like it. The audience screamed their heads off and danced, danced, and danced, crowding the stage for a closer look at these fabulous rock and rollers. They were wild for the Beatles. The reaction was so dramatic it could have been operatic; their version of the Isley Brothers' 'Twist and Shout' created a sensation. Beatlemania? Well, most certainly the start of it. And their Cavern days were beginning. George wrote to Stuart, telling him: 'Some queer bloke was almost on his knees, asking me if we could play for him.'

When Stuart returned to Liverpool, in the middle of January 1961, the Beatles were playing almost daily, often two venues an evening. John was delighted to see Stuart. It was mutual. He came round to the house and they talked for hours and hours: it was as if they had never been apart. Stuart wanted to know what was happening in Liverpool and John wanted all the gossip from the Reeperbahn, what the girls were up to – and who was up to the girls. They were going to take me to the Cavern but I had to wait and wait until they had finished talking.

They went out the door that night like Siamese twins – with me in tow. When we got to the Cavern, Paul was not so friendly and George, despite his pleading letter only a month earlier, looked as though he had swallowed some bad medicine. Paul was now quite accomplished on the bass and George more than the others wanted to keep the status quo. They had sensed they were going somewhere and Stuart and ambition were in conflict for them. John was adamant about the return of his best friend: if he goes, I go. That evening, before I was taken home by Stuart and he returned for a night out with John and the others, the atmosphere seemed to get better. It had to or there would have been the most almighty bust-up, and the story of the Beatles would most probably have ended there and then.

The matter was dropped. Stuart was back in the line-up and in February 1961 appeared with the others as a Beatle at the Cavern; only John had played there before, in 1957 with the Quarrymen.

Never shy of experiences, my mother went to the Cavern. After Stuart's death she was asked in a radio interview about this and said: 'I admit I went down very prejudiced and prepared to be utterly disgusted – I mean, I was very much older than their generation. But I was absolutely astounded. It was delightful, I thoroughly enjoyed them. They really were great.'

And they were. I saw them at the Cavern and they were all much, much better – not just the singing and stage antics but the coordination between them. Their confidence was absolute, for they knew they had that little something extra, whatever that magical 'it' is that set them apart from all those scores of other Merseyside groups – and, as we all found, from *every* other group.

But Paul and George were still not happy with Stuart on bass and they constantly questioned his commitment; they had good reason to. The main object of Stuart's return had not been to rejoin the band. He had come back and was living at home, like the other boys, but in his case to prepare for a 23 February interview at art school. He had excitedly told me about the work Astrid's friends were involved in at Hamburg's State School of Fine Art. He wanted to keep his word to our mother about going back to his studies in September, but it was clear to me he missed painting and Astrid. It must have been galling for Paul and George, who had their fingertips on their dreams, especially when Stuart applied for a visa to return to Germany. Back in England, Stuart wrote to Ken Horton. This is an exact copy of the letter:

> *Tonight a priest snugly wrapped in a 30gn Savile Row coat said 'good night' to me, before I knew what I was saying my nerves said the same. Then the bus I was waiting for, didn't and almost in the second I was cursing. And meanwhile I'm sitting by my cheap electric fire (my mother's really, and certainly her shillings) in my horrible green pajamas, and from the seething of my stampeded thoughts comes a strange harmony, which I like because it is full of a humming noise. sometimes it hisses like piss in a urinal or a cat cornered in the ruins,*

sometimes it's like the wrangling of angels (there are such things, I've seen one), when the sky opens in summer lightning and flames, such flames that burn the soul and you jump back terrified.

And this Angel I saw was a rhinoceros, with glasses, typical national health specimen, obviously dying of cancer, but I knew it was an angel because it had wings. And then of course my Hamburg angels – and devils, one I thought was a devil disguised as a guitar, but he turned out to be nothing more than an old harp. See we are deceived by things!! And this Liverpool that is a brass coffin, but they skimped a bit on the handles and they came off, so now we can't lower it into the pit, and the worms and the bugs crawl slowly upwards.

I stand void of pleasures, for I have forsaken this place. Hamburg and Astrid. I was crushed by the rock of her irresistible weight, my heart fluttered like a frightened bird, my alcoves were flooded with radiance and I was swept away like a light feather. For many nights, I had prepared for this, I had washed the windows of my soul and in silence oiled the door to my heart. Oh how can I help being bored! In the sky above the earth shines a million stars, each one glittering in a different way, and everything is stationary. Astrid. Dear Ken, how sad for you that I write so, forgive me that I use you as the harp on which I play my comic-opera.

Writing this 1 week later, I find myself reminded of the sailor who fell off the crow's nest into the hold, where there was a cargo of rubber. He starved to death, because the crew couldn't pass him any food during the three days he bounced up and down. I was related that story by an old sailor while I was working on the bins, and despite its improbability, it has remarkable associations with the stranglehold which the routine of everyday life has on us. Surely I'm bounced up and down so much in the last few months. I must have died but I feel remarkably keen. Don't worry, I don't intend allowing my talent to go to seed while I'm here in Liverpool. I intend starting a play, Mr Man and Queen Elsie. Mr Man is a bus-conductor and Queenie is his subconscious inspector, quite difficult but it will be a little absorbing – I think. I hate Liverpool in all its trivialities, believe me Ken, don't

take any of the staff seriously, they lead such a closeted existence.
I think this letter is a bit negative so I'll finish.

Stuart was a little lost. John pulled him back into the Beatles and there was much work: they were booked solid, for six and eight pounds an appearance, for the first quarter of 1961. It was like being back in Hamburg, session after session after session. Neil Aspinall, a good friend of Pete Best and his mother's lodger, gave up accountancy to be the Beatles' road manager, their first roadie. In a Commer van they and their equipment criss-crossed the Mersey-beat town and dance halls. Some of these places were terrifying. George and Paul were beaten up at Hambleton Hall in Huyton, and Stuart received a severe beating at Lathom Hall, Seaforth, Liverpool, on 30 January 1961. The group were helping Neil Aspinall load equipment through a fire door at the back of the stage and into their van. Stuart was on his own when he looked up and there were a crowd of toughs. They had waited until John and the others had gone back inside the hall. Stuart said he was punched in the stomach so hard he rolled on to the ground and his glasses fell from his face. He had one hand on his head and the other between his legs as he was kicked and punched.

John was alerted by a couple of girls and rushed out to help. He ran into the thugs and the punching and kicking went on. John sprained his wrist and broke his finger and it might have been much worse but Pete Best, the true hard man of the group, arrived and the odds became too intimidating for the hooligans, who ran off. Pete remembered: 'John and I doubled back and charged into the fray, freeing Stu and collecting our fair share of knocks along the way. Lennon broke a finger belting a Ted and had to play guitar for a while wearing a splint.' Stuart's face was smothered in blood. He came home to us at the flat we had moved to at 53 Ullet Road, overlooking Sefton Park. He collapsed in the doorway, all battered and bleeding. By then there was bruising all over his forehead; it was if someone had painted it black and blue. My mother was horrified at first but then was quite calm about the attack. She got on with making Stuart comfortable and wanted to call the doctor but Stuart said no. The next morning my mother called the doctor anyway. The advice was a couple of days in bed. Stuart got up and my mother said to me: 'He has no time to be ill – he's too fond of life.'

And Astrid. Stuart and I talked a lot at this time. But not about the attack. He seemed to get over it quickly, back to normal almost immediately. There certainly did not appear to be any debilitating damage and after many years of study and investigation I have found nothing to connect this fight with Stuart's early demise. With me, the youngest sister, he was always cheerful. He had come back to see the boys, get the band together, get on with his painting, but he also used to take me out a lot with him; we had many conversations and I would hear more about Astrid. He would go with me to buy new clothes and helped chose them. Of course, he would talk about Astrid and her fashions and style. She had sent us photographs of herself before we met her so we knew that she was quite extraordinarily beautiful. She still has that charismatic quality about her, but then she was quite exceptional.

I was seventeen years old when Astrid came over. She brought my sister and me a pair of Dior stockings each as gifts; a Liverpool girl, despite all the tastefulness and culture in my household, I had never seen a pair of Dior stockings in my whole life. I thought they were the most exquisite things I could ever have, see, and feel. She brought a single orchid for my mother and so that laid down a marker; what an extraordinarily interesting gift, one orchid, not a whopping huge bouquet. Impressive. We were impressed, my sister and me. We had all been nervous in the house, anticipating her visit with some trepidation. Stuart was silent, very contained. I think he was frightened of the reaction of my mother. He and Astrid knew from her letters that she thought Stuart was too young to marry – he's got his whole life ahead of him. He had written to my father who had regretted his first, young marriage. Stuart reminded my father that he did not get permission when he first got engaged and he was just doing the same. My father, graciously, did not write back and say that he repented at leisure about the error he made; he didn't remind Stuart of that. It was an astonishing situation for my mother and father: their son is leading this amazingly decadent life, he's got this extraordinary beautiful girlfriend who is not a totty or anything but from this established middle-class background. She's an educated young woman, a very okay girl in terms of bringing the future bride home. It should be a walkover but the big factor was that he was so young. I think there were echoes in there from my parents that they never mentioned what had happened to my father. There was all of that, although it was not expressed openly to me or my sister.

Also, I think my mother spotted something in Astrid when they met. It wasn't joy.

My mother and Stuart had some long looks and difficult words with each other. I never heard the arguments and neither of them would ever talk about them, but I have to believe it was all about Astrid. My mother and brother – they'd go off like that at each other and then heal, a little bit like John and Auntie Mimi. This time it seemed different to me; you felt you could play tunes on the tension lines.

Although my mother knew they shared the annexe rooms at Astrid's mother's home, she had no intention of allowing them to sleep together at 53 Ullet Road. Her open mind only went so far, and we had only just slipped into the 1960s. Stuart and Astrid left and went and stayed with Allan and Beryl Williams. It gave Stuart the chance he wanted to show off the leather-suited girl on his arm. Veronica Johnson met them at art school and thought Stuart seemed very happy. Susan Williams met them by chance in Lewis's department store and invited them to her twenty-first birthday party immediately before Valentine's Day. Stuart told her that he had burned her love letters to him at Astrid's request, so it was no surprise that they did not turn up for her celebrations. Philip Hartas knew from the college grapevine about the blonde woman Stuart had found in Hamburg and called her 'a beautiful creature' when he met her. Bill Harry met Stuart in the Jacaranda and found him changed: 'He didn't seem to talk about music at all. He talked about philosophy and the deep things – I thought he'd turned into an existentialist. He was with Astrid, they were both dressed completely in black, and both white as a sheet. Stuart seemed more withdrawn, less forthcoming, than he'd ever been before. He was into Kierkegaard – he had the book in his pocket and showed me.'

At home we had noticed hints of this new Stuart, but nothing like Bill Harry reported. Stuart just seemed to have grown up in Germany and for me that was different – he was the man in our family with our father away so much. Stuart then got a shock that changed his direction and thinking. The college interview on 23 February went badly and he was rejected for his teaching course. He was furious and took his attitude out on Nicholas Horsfield, who had taught him in the college's painting school and knew him well. Nicholas was astounded: 'He came to ask me to recommend him for the teaching course, and I refused for two reasons. The first was that I wanted to dissuade him – I did that to everybody who was any good. It would have been no good for him as an artist, and frustrating for him as a person. But also he didn't go about it in the way one usually asked for a recommendation. I remember being surprised, taken aback, by his aggressive manner – he practically demanded a recommendation. Maybe I was a bit biased – he came waltzing in with his winklepicker shoes on.' It was after this incident that Stuart told Ken Horton: '. . . this Liverpool that is a brass coffin, but they skimped a bit on the handles and they came off, so now we can't lower it into the pit, and the worms and bugs crawl slowly upwards.'

He was upset. In addition, Stuart had been used to getting whatever he wanted – at home from my mother, at college from his indulgent tutors who in their way also wanted to mother him. Until this time he had received nothing but encouragement and praise at college. This part of growing up he took badly and saw his salvation – and Astrid – back in Germany. Which is where the Beatles were also heading. Peter Eckhorn, who owned the Top Ten and had helped Pete Best retrieve the equipment left by the group after their sudden departure from Hamburg, had arranged for them to play his club in April. Visas were arranged, deportation orders rescinded, and other immigration problems solved, and what was to become a marathon – 503 hours onstage over 92 nights – contracted. Stuart was the Beatles' point man. He left via the Newhaven ferry and Harwich on 15 March 1961, a couple of weeks before the rest of the troops.

Stuart and Astrid visited the police in Hamburg to ensure that all was in order for the rest of the Beatles to return. George was eighteen and entitled to be there, as was John who had left Germany voluntarily. Stuart pledged the future good behaviour of Paul and Pete, and Stuart wrote to Pete: 'The lifting of a deportation ban is only valid for 1 year, then you can have it renewed. One thing they made clear, if you have any trouble with the Police, no matter how small, you've had it forever. (Drunkenness, fighting, women etc.)'

It was April Fool's Day when John and the others arrived at the Top Ten, but there were no pranks. The bad blood between Stuart and Paul and George was clear from the start. Stuart sat in with them and Jurgen Vollmer regularly watched the performances and analysed Stuart's attitude for me: 'His heart was no longer in it. I'm sure he never had any kind of ambition to become a rock and roll musician. When onstage he always seemed in another world – completely the dreamer. The others would be giving it their all, but Stuart just did it because it was the thing to do at the time. As I saw it, John was his best friend. There was nothing other than harmony between them. I remember that sometimes Paul and George would look critically at Stuart, presumably when he wasn't playing well – but although I've always loved rock and roll I'm not a musician, so I couldn't judge his playing.'

Tony Sheridan said he always felt Stuart was playing the wrong instrument: 'It looked very strange, this small chap with an amazingly big bass. Stuart wasn't really a guitarist or a singer, and he obviously wasn't a drummer. Maybe today, with all the technological possibilities, he would have found a way. But I feel his involvement was really that of a catalyst. He wasn't interested in being in the limelight as a musician. He was more interested in what was going on, and very interested in being a part of that in a sort of roundabout way, on the periphery.'

I suspect part of the problem was that Paul saw Stuart as an interloper in his relationship with John for, as he would see it, he was there first. As Paul said to me: 'Looking back on it now, I think it was little tinges of jealousy because Stu was John's friend. There was always a little jealousy among the group as to who would be John's friend. He was like the guy you aspired to.'

Thus, Stuart's skills as a bass guitarist became more and more of an issue. It certainly provided a more acceptable excuse for the arguments and tantrums. Paul told me: 'We could actually go to an audition and not make too many mistakes but Stu – I did feel that he was holding us back musically. It was the same with Peter Best, in fact. Stuart and I would have our set-tos, but not many. The major one – and I don't remember what triggered it – was a fight on stage. It wasn't actually a fight because neither of us were good fighters, it was more of a grapple. I remember thinking: "Well, he's littler than me, I'll easily floor him." But this guy had the strength of ten men. So there we were, me and Stu, grunting and locked together in this sort of death embrace, and all the gangsters [in the audience] laughing at us and shouting, "C'mon, hit him." ' Then Paul softened his recollection of the relationship, telling me: 'But Stu lent me his bass guitar when he left the group, so obviously we liked each other well enough, basically. I remember a string broke on that guitar and we couldn't get new strings – it must have been a Sunday or something – so we just got some pliers, and took an A string off the piano, and amazingly it worked.'

In Paul's version the fight is all shrugged off as a lark between friends. But Pete Best's version of the fight indicates that Paul had taunted Stuart: 'Breaking point came one night when we were backing Tony Sheridan at the Top Ten. Paul was at the piano as usual for Tony's act when he said something about Astrid that must have really hurt. Stu had been used to harmless ribbing, which frayed his temper occasionally; it usually stopped when he protested but whatever Paul said that night really struck home. Although normally something of a pacifist, this time Stu dropped the bass guitar, stormed across the stage to the piano and landed Paul such a wallop that it knocked him off his stool. Paul and Stu began struggling on the floor of the stand, rolling round locked in the most ferocious battle. Tony began to dry up, but then he recovered and began to shout his lyrics. Paul and Stu fought on for around five minutes – until the number ended and we prised them apart to applause from the audience. They were accustomed to John and Paul's mock battles in the cause of making show but I doubt if any of them could have fooled themselves into believing that this was all part of the act. When battle had ceased, Stu raged at Paul: "Don't you ever say anything about Astrid again, or I'll beat the brains out of you." "I'll say what I like," Paul yelled back. They argued on and off for the rest of the night; it was the beginning of the end for Stu as a Beatle: the crunch had arrived.'

Astrid was acutely observant of all the rows. In Philip Norman's acclaimed Beatles biography *Shout!* he quotes her saying: 'When John and Stu had a row you could still feel the affection that was there. But when Paul and Stu had a row, you could tell Paul hated him.'

George also was no longer a fan. He had run-ins with Stuart: 'I had a lot of fist fights with Stu but I really liked him and we were very friendly before he died. I suppose the reason I was fighting with him was that in the ego pecking order, he wasn't really a musician. He was in the band because John had conned him into buying a bass. He was like our Art Director. In a mysterious way

Stuart, in conjunction with the German crowd, not just Astrid, was really responsible for that certain look we had.'

That was all true, and Stuart told me he was only staying with the group and sitting in with them because of John. John, he said, relied on him, and I have to wonder if John in his mischievous way did keep Stuart around just to mix it up with the others. But that thought is overtaken when I study the evidence of John's vehement reaction to Stuart's announcement in June 1961 that he was going to go to art college in Hamburg and was therefore leaving the Beatles for good.

At this time the hugely successful record producer Bert Kaempfert, who had co-written Elvis's 'Wooden Heart', had arranged for the Beatles to back Tony Sheridan in the recording of five songs, including one that was to be pivotal for them, the rock version of 'My Bonnie Lies Over the Ocean'. The Beatles received a standard session rate, no royalties, for what was a successful record for Sheridan – and thereafter a prized Beatles collectors' commodity. Stuart did not play on the session at the Friedrich Ebert Halle in Hamburg, but he was there for all the recordings. He was there for John. His letters to me had always been full of information about the music and the audience reaction, about the bickering between Paul and George and John and Pete Best and himself. His gossipy life, in his letters, revolved around the group and what was happening with them. Now, he rarely mentioned the Beatles or anything about them. Psychologically, he had left the group.

His mind, as the others were so angrily aware of, was elsewhere. He still had to tell John he did not want to make the show any more. He eventually did and much agonizing and acrimony resulted from his decision. John had fought for Stuart's place in the band and supported him over Paul and George's complaints. Stuart told me that John was offended by his decision to quit the Beatles. Stuart said there was much heartbreak, contradicting what has been reported over the years. After all these hours on the bass with the Beatles, Stuart was not booted out because he could not play the right chords on a guitar. It was always more than that. In the event they all dealt with it, on the surface, like gentlemen.

Pete Best, who had his own nightmares to contend with, said in his tactful, pleasant way about Stuart leaving the group: 'His exit was all cut and dried in one night. No dithering, no soul-searching, no postponing, and no bitterness.'

On paper, in his letters, Stuart's words were all about his love of art and Astrid. In April he had written to my mother: 'I'm still a bit sad you think I've made a mess of my future, but out of it all I have something to really compensate – my love for Astrid, which knows no bounds, and her love for me. I'm quite certain I will start a teaching course in September and hope to learn for definite where in the next two or three months.'

But by then something had happened that would begin Stuart's slow, agonizing death. Which I believe John Lennon was inadvertently responsible for. Just as I believe that John was haunted by Stuart's death for the rest of his life.

eight

Torture

'To the very end, Stu Sutcliffe had lived out
the myth of the "poète maudit".'

Albert Goldman in *The Lives of John Lennon*

Saturday May

Dear Mum, thanks for your beautiful
letters which we got yesterday!
I thought I'd wait till you were
settling in before writing in reply. It
gave a surprise to find you moving
again although no doubt for the better,
but a little guilty that perhaps I was
instrumental in landing you with
a white elephant.
Thanks for all that you are doing
for me. I still wonder at the thought
of me, inc. Astrid has completely
altered the blue one, it is now absolutely

2

beautiful, and I don't think you will
think the trousers too tight – their
beautiful and without pocket. My
beauty and I had a good
laugh at the thought of Paytine
coming to the cavern with the
photo. I hope they were all
sincere, but when we come we
will go and see the Beatles. We've
heard from Gerry that they are all
doing so good now, Gerry isn't
any good as a band.
I think you must have your hands
full with the house – I don't envy the
task

3

My doctor here is on holiday and,
won't return till about the 16th of May.
I don't think this is too late, so we'll
wait till then
I know this boy Cottinge, I used to
like him very much, although he
was a bit older than me, but I liked
his work very much. He was definitely
superior to the others, and I have no
doubt superior to McKinley, whose work
I also know. I know Cottinge was of
better means than most, his father died
a few years ago.

x

feel better now, although no doubt
about it my nerves were pretty
bad and although worse I'm only
smoking about 6 cigarettes a day
now and have done for about 2
weeks, although he substituted chewing
gum for them. Anyway all my love to
you and the family from Astrid and
I (she's as marvellous as you say)
your loving son, Stuart. xxxx.

JOHN AND PAUL had to ease up on the local attractions at Easter in 1961 when Cynthia and Paul's on-and-off girlfriend Dot Rhone arrived in Hamburg for a holiday. The girls stayed with Astrid and her mother. Astrid was very fond of Cynthia and took her and Dot on a tourist trip of the city and to all the best shops. If Cynthia didn't have something to wear for the evening, Astrid would gleefully produce something from her own wardrobe. Cynthia has always been careful and in a situation like this would have been inhibited. But she got into the spirit of it and they seemed to have a lot of fun together. Astrid would take them on a drive to Ostsee, which is a beach resort – I have lovely photographs of Stuart and John, if not exactly building sandcastles, attempting some sand-based architecture. Stuart's wearing a silly hat and has a half-smoked cigarette in one photograph of him and John. In another he has that hat on and is gazing out at the water. That was his summer of 1961, his last summer. It doesn't seem possible, for he looks so self-assured, so in control in the photographs. I presume he felt his life was on track: he had Astrid, he was going back to his art work, therefore pleasing his parents, and John was being a terrific friend. Stuart was also having fun with fashion. The James Dean rocker image was getting a mellow makeover.

Astrid would wear his leather jacket while he wore her collarless blouse, knotted at the front and displaying his lean if not six-pack figure. He always wore the mock-crocodile winklepickers from England. Klaus loved them and wanted a pair. Stuart did a cardboard cut-out of Klaus's foot, and sent it to Mother to go and buy him a pair of grey, artificial-crocodile boots – the same as Stuart's. Klaus has said that his relationship with Astrid was more like siblings when Stuart came into the picture, so it was no emotional upheaval for him. Stuart and Klaus liked each other, but I suspect that below the surface there were undercurrents or unresolved issues. Klaus and Astrid wrote a book for Genesis Publications, which is based in Surrey and is associated with George Harrison. In that book, Klaus makes the point about Stuart not having been one of Astrid's clones but someone who had kept his own identity and sense of self even if he had been restyled by Astrid. This suggests to me that Stuart resolved the doubts for himself, yet Astrid and Klaus have returned to one another, on and off, throughout their adult lives, which is interesting and intriguing.

The other member of the Hamburg trio that Stuart encountered, Jurgen Vollmer, holds a fiercely different attitude. In several conversations I have had with him in London, he became incandescent at the mere mention of Astrid's name. He behaved like a man carrying a very deep wound and seemed to be reluctant to let it heal. It may be that he felt he should have the credit for creating the Beatles' haircut, but I suspect there is much more than that involved. As well as being a stylish photographer he was also something of a Vidal Sassoon and he did cut John and Paul's hair in Paris just as he shaped his own in that mop, combed-forward style. But John and Paul were later converts.

Stuart and Astrid were also wearing leather trousers that were almost like drainies, drainpipe jeans: you didn't need an imagination, for they were so form hugging. John, Paul, George, and Pete were also entranced by the leather pants, which echoed the style of Gene Vincent and Eddie Cochran, their teenage rock idols. They all bought pairs; but at first they were having nothing to do with Stuart's mop-style, brushed-forward long hair.

Stuart striking a moody pose for this self-portrait, Hamburg 1961.
(Pauline Sutcliffe collection)

The Sutcliffe line-up. Stuart, me, Joyce
and our mother, Millie, in 1947.

My father Charles,
also in 1947.

Looking at the future: Stuart at Prescott Grammer School, front row, second from the right.
(all pictures from the Pauline Sutcliffe collection)

ABOVE LEFT Anarchy and beer: Stuart having a pint at the Cracke pub, 1958. (courtesy of Rod Murray)

ABOVE Stuart by the infamous new fireplace in Percy Street, with one of his paintings above. (courtesy of Rod Murray)

OPPOSITE John and Cynthia in Liverpool. This is how I like to remember them – young, happy, with so much talent. (Pauline Sutcliffe collection courtesy of Cynthia Lennon and Phyllis MacKenzie)

Auditioning for Larry Parnes
in 1960. Stuart is turned away,
in a characteristic pose.
(Pauline Sutcliffe collection)

Posing on stage at the Indra –
from left to right: John, George,
Pete, Paul and Stuart in his
shades, the James Dean of
Hamburg. (courtesy Pete Best)

The Beatles on stage at the Indra.
(courtesy Pete Best)

Waiting to go on at the Indra, Stuart and John togeth
on the left. (Pauline Sutcliffe collection)

This horrible foto of Astrid and me at the festival, with Klaus friend of Astrid and me. He looks much better than that Beatleg, Actually this is the second day, so you can imagine how we felt, I was plastered at the time

A13 + A14

(Pauline Sutcliffe collection)

Jurgen took this portrait of Astrid and Stuart in Hamburg, and it shows the artistic mood of the times. (courtesy of Jurgen Vollmer)

Crossed guitars: Stuart and John perhaps discussing the existentialist elements of rock 'n' roll on stage in Hamburg. (Pauline Sutcliffe collection)

I adore this happy photograph
of John and Stuart creating
sand 'art' at the beach, 1961.
(Pauline Sutcliffe collection)

Stuart was in a serious
mood when he took this
self portrait and it recalls
for me that side of him.
(Pauline Sutcliffe collection)

Meeting up with Astrid in Japan for the release of *Backbeat*. (Pauline Sutcliffe)

The Rock and Roll Hall of Fame in Cleveland, Ohio, in 2001. There's Stuart on his poster – out of view is John; he has been with us for most of our lives, always part of Stuart's story. (Pauline Sutcliffe)

Freeze-framed for ever young. Astrid took this photograph of Stuart in 1961.
I still love him. We all do. (Astrid Kirchherr/Redferns)

When Stuart first appeared in the Top Ten with his hair restyled by Astrid, the other four reacted with noisy derision. According to Jurgen, George was the first of the other Beatles to follow suit and brush his hair forwards into a heavy fringe – although when the Rockers gave him funny looks he swept it back again for a while before adopting the new style permanently. John and Paul held out for a few months longer: Jurgen had moved to Paris and was involved with a Bohemian crowd. John and Paul hitch-hiked from Liverpool to visit him at the Hôtel du Beaune, on the Left Bank. The girls in Jurgen's circle were not impressed, turned on, by the rocker look of John and Paul, and they correctly thought they had a better chance with the girls if they achieved the softer and more literary Left Bank look. Jurgen reported: 'I gave them the haircut in my room. Then, their hair was just like Stuart's.'

The Beatles' style was evolving. Only Pete Best, dignified and always his own man, a true individual who sadly lost out on so much of the fortune and fame, always resisted Stuart's Beatles hair-style. He was also the one who avoided the drugs on offer in Hamburg, the pill-popping that kept Stuart and the others raving through the night. When the Beatles were in Hamburg in 1961 Preludin tablets, known on the street as prellies, were as available as a packet of cigarettes. They worked fast, like a car accelerator, exhaustion to energy in sixty seconds. Preludin is amphetamine-related and stimulates the nervous system. It is used to relieve depression and control obesity. It is not a drug to be prescribed for Stuart, who was underweight. Or to John, who had his own built-in accelerator. The drug's known side effects include headaches, insomnia, restlessness, and disorientation; tolerance is quick, addiction prevalent. I cannot say what other drugs they were using, but many were available. When you have taken one pill it is easy to move on to others, to seek more kicks or effect, something to get you to sleep, something else to keep you going.

The Beatles were playing hour after hour after hour. John was taking all the pills and all the booze on offer. As I said, part of the rationale for the uppers and downers was because they played day and night, seven days a week.

John was known to overdrink to the point of madness or coma. If he didn't collapse he would get violent and smash the place up as well as other people. He was always hard to handle. Excessive. John did it to excess. It also made him jealous. He did not want anyone else to have Stuart. Astrid was a threat – and, of course, he fancied Astrid himself. She was another blonde, but foreign and exotic. What added the frisson was that Stuart had her. Paul and George meanwhile were complaining about Stuart's musical abilities. In John's mind he probably mixed that up with Stuart's sexual talents, and all the jealousies fermented from that, for Stuart was so special to John. So, imagine John's mind. He is getting pressure from all directions. Stuart knew all about this and told me of it the last time I saw him, which was when he came to see my mother in the early part of 1962.

He also told me about the fight with John. He was not more precise in detail about the time and place other than it was in May 1961, and in the street and near the Top Ten. John was complaining to him about what Paul and George had been saying: Stuart looked miserable onstage – if he turned up – and he would walk offstage to talk to Astrid; Stuart was never going to get any better on bass, for he wasn't trying. It was all an irritating fanfare in John's mind, according to Stuart. He said John did not want the aggravation, he wanted to maintain the status quo. But Stuart wanted to go off with Astrid, go off and paint, to leave the Beatles, to desert John. John envied Stuart's choices, as the perceptive Tony Sheridan noticed. He could choose to go back to art school.

Indeed, Stuart and John had discussed the possibility of them both leaving the Beatles, continuing their beautiful friendship, and resuming their art studies in Liverpool. What if John had?

Instead, late one evening it all got out of control. It was John at his most random. He and Stuart were talking in the street in Hamburg and suddenly Stuart was lying on the pavement having been punched by John. He had no time to even attempt to protect himself. The brakes weren't working for John and he was taken over by one of his uncontrollable rages: he kicked out at Stuart again and again and kicked him in the head. There was blood streaming down from Stuart's head when John finally came to his senses. John looked down at Stuart – and fled, disgusted and terrified by his attack. He could not confront what he had done. Paul McCartney was with them when the fight began but could do nothing to stop the instant, insane burst of violence. Paul helped Stuart, who was bleeding from his face and ear, and took him back to their rooms. John wasn't there but turned up later. John never talked to Stuart about it – John rarely went back to pick up the pieces resulting from his dreadful behaviour.

Stuart was lost by the immediacy and violence of the moment. He had been frightened of John's losing it with others but had always felt immune because John loved him; Stuart saw himself as the peacekeeper, the one who calmed John down. But it had turned into a violent riot, with John flailing and kicking out at Stuart.

One clue to why my brother died came from the doctors, who said there was an indent in the front of his skull, medically explained as the result of a 'trauma' – meaning a knock or a kick. In all the many official records and books about the Beatles this event is not mentioned, but I know Stuart and John had a fight because Stuart told me. He told me they had a fallout and John had beaten him up. Stuart said it was all over in moments. John went crazy – he couldn't even remember what they were talking about other than it was not anything controversial. He said John had been brooding as they walked along but they were such good friends that they did not need to be constantly making conversation. Then, like a volcano, John blew up. Stuart did not know anything until he was splayed across the pavement. He said he could smell the streets, the debris of them; that was the only sense he had as John kicked him again and again. Stuart said it hurt terribly but he was too surprised and shocked to truly feel the damage that was being inflicted on him.

Stuart said John kicked him in the head, and I'm convinced that kick was what eventually led to Stuart's death. John stayed silent. My mother was dogged for the rest of her life by how Stuart had died. Why should a healthy young man develop such awful symptoms – then suddenly die?

I know John always held himself responsible for Stuart dying. I learned much later that he told Yoko Ono about the fight in Hamburg. Yoko Ono told a friend, Marnie Hair, what John had said about his guilt at losing control with Stuart and punching and kicking him. John had told Yoko he was wearing his gold and silver cowboy boots with pointed toes, the ones Aunt Mimi hated, during the fight.

I feel terrible for John – how must it have felt to so badly hurt someone you loved? And then he could have had no idea of the repercussions, of what he had done. I cannot say for certain when he first realized, but he must have suspected when he heard how Stuart had died. Especially, after all the investigations. All the headaches and pain that he knew Stuart went through. In the film *Backbeat* the confrontation is presented as bloody but in a bloody-nose sort of way: fisticuffs that end in a tearful hug. That was not even close to what really happened, with John running away, terrified of what he'd done to Stuart.

Of course, that confrontation changed their relationship but no one else would have realized that. They wrote long letters to each other right up to Stuart's death. I think Stuart simply accepted that this violence was part of John's character, John's problems, and Stuart wanted even more to look after him. Although John had physically hurt Stuart, it was Stuart who wanted to protect John, guard him from himself if nothing else. That might have been arrogant of Stuart, believing that he was the only one who could fulfil that role. But of all the letters and material I have I cannot refer to John's letters to Stuart and Stuart's to John at this time.

Astrid gave John his letters to Stuart and I presume they are now held by Yoko. Where are Stuart's letters to John and what did they write about? There may have been an explanation there for what made John lose control so terribly and so devastatingly with Stuart.

Stuart had fallen in love with Astrid and left the Beatles and gone back to his art: John had all sorts of emotions boiling over. It was a moment of madness, a blackout of conscience, but when he calmed down John would have had everything sorted and filed in his memory bank. He would have known what had happened. And that is the torture – the replay, the constant replay, always there in his head. Easier to take heroin in later years and block so much out.

After that awful encounter with John, the first significant signs that something was wrong with Stuart that our family saw was with the arrival of his letters; his handwriting, which was usually a smallish, slanting, and slightly italic script looked looped, upright and very large. Later, photographs would arrive showing him getting thinner and thinner. He wrote to us about his weight loss on 10 July 1961, about a week after the Beatles had returned to Liverpool, but said he would fatten up and did not dwell on it.

Stuart was spending a lot of time at the Top Ten and I suspect popping pills for the pain and to keep him going. He wrote to us about spending his days painting and sculpting at Astrid's. Tony Sheridan recalled for me his memories of the summer of 1961 and said how protective Astrid was of Stuart: 'She really looked after him. It was a very violent place yet she managed to keep him a bit apart from the violence. I don't know how she did it, but she had a way of speaking to people that commanded respect from all types. Astrid was much more than a girl we all fell in love with. She was a catalyst, her effect on everybody was such that it brought out the best in them, musically as well as personally. It was a very, very magical atmosphere in Hamburg at that time – and very important for the musical scene in Britain. We had a sort of cocoon of very creative people involved with music and art, and Stuart was a large part of that, and all the time the violence and red-light stuff was going on all around us. I think John was in a way proud to be a product of the Liverpool art scene, but he wanted to be both sides of the fence, a Jack-the-Lad, as well as an intellectual. He didn't respect anybody without reason but he respected Stuart, as a dedicated artist and as a personality. It was important to John to be a part of the arty scene in Hamburg, and I think he was grateful to Stuart and Astrid for making it possible for him to have that sort of status.'

My mother received an important letter, written in two parts, from Stuart at the end of May:

> John Hart has written telling me I have all his support and Arthur
> Ballard's when I wish to teach. He's very happy that I have started
> to paint again. Yes I have started and things are going quite nicely, in
> a few weeks I should have a grip on myself. My pictures are not
> abstract now, vaguely figurative and mostly blue.
>
> You might have seen in the paper that a top English sculptor is
> now teaching in the big college here, Paolozzi (he comes from
> Edinburgh). Anyway tomorrow I'm going to the college to start
> drawing again for 3 days a week. I've seen an assistant director and he
> said he'll turn a blind eye, then when Paolozzi comes I must speak
> with him about staying in his class for a while (Astrid is beautiful and
> lovely and wonderful as always and we are so very happy together). It
> all depends on this Paolozzi man, but I might go to college for a year,
> with a grant. Although it's vague yet, this can be a tremendous fillip
> to my reputation when I return to England.

Stuart waited to send the letter, and when he did it concluded with the news that he was to meet Eduardo Paolozzi at the college on the following Monday: 'Could you send my certificates and things because if I'm going to enrol at the college I'll need them, you can't imagine how important it will be for me to have a good reference from this man.'

The phraseology of his written English was becoming notice-ably Germanic after several months' exposure to the language and culture. A note he wrote in mid-May to enclose with gifts for his parents could easily be mistaken for the work of a German whose English is reasonably fluent, but formal and unidiomatic. This is particularly apparent in his use of 'when' in place of 'if', which is *wenn* in German: 'Dear Mum. Here's a little thing for you. When you don't like it or it's too small or something you must send it back quickly and I can change it. I thought the colour would suit you best, but don't be frightened of saying when you don't like it. The other is for my father for his birthday, please give this to him for me. I think he will like this big thing. I will write another letter soon. Love from Astrid and me. Your son Stuart.'

On 23 June 1961, it was twenty-one years since Stuart had been born at the Simpson Memorial Maternity Pavilion in Edinburgh and Hitler was viewing his conquests in Paris. The Top Ten club in Hamburg was the last place any of us could have anticipated Stuart celebrating such a landmark birthday. All his friends knew about it but for some reason Astrid freaked out when Jurgen arrived at the club with a bouquet of roses for Stuart: 'We were young and artistic and it was a gesture we considered chic. Bringing roses was to us just a sign of admiration, nothing more. But Astrid was furious, because she didn't want anyone to know it was Stuart's birthday. I had actually put the roses behind the piano, but after she and I had the dispute over my gift, I went behind the piano and destroyed them. Then John got a little nasty, as he sometimes could, and said that they hadn't all been my roses because he had bought some too. So I told him, very arrogantly, that I had only destroyed my bouquet.'

It is clear that the fences had only been mended on the surface. Stuart's headaches, which had started a couple of weeks earlier, became more frequent. I think Astrid must have sensed that something was not right with Stuart. His letters indicate that she was getting more and more impatient with his tiredness, his constant lack of energy, get-up-and-go. She was the one who encouraged him to go to the Top Ten to see the Beatles. Stuart *wanted* to go but Astrid, according to her letters, had to energize him. She thought that Stuart being with and seeing his friends perform would help get him out of his malady. According to Astrid, Stuart was always more cheerful when he saw the boys and it must have helped her too, for it cannot have been much fun having to cope with such an ill person all the time.

They went almost every night to the Top Ten until John and the others left for Liverpool on 2 July. After a two-week break they were soaring on Merseyside and Cavern regulars. Stuart obviously knew something was wrong, but in the weeks that followed he gave us conflicting stories: he would be feeling awful and by the next letter happily well. In a letter written two weeks after his birthday, Stuart responded to my mother's remarks about his weight loss:

I know I'm thin but hope to be fatter soon. Anyway could you please send me my blue suit and old grey shoes (for working in). I have written to Allan Williams telling him I want an exhibition in Sept. of my new pictures. I will be coming home then for a couple of weeks holiday.

I had a lovely letter from my father about a week ago, and have replied to his American address. Now I'm having a short break before starting painting again. I shall also find a job for a few weeks to strengthen funds etc. Perhaps Joyce and Pauline will get round to writing 1 day.

All is beautiful here as always and I'm settling down comfortably. I'm still nervous and excited this is why I can't settle properly to write to you, I hope you forgive me. But lots of love to all and more to you than the others. Your son (your young man), Stuart.

It was a terrible time for all of us, but especially my mother. On the one hand she's trying to stand back and let Stuart be independent, and on the other she wants to go and grab him in her arms and get him home. She also got trapped in Stuart's contradictions; first he's terribly ill, and then he's much better today. We were puzzled and confused at this point. I was seventeen going on eighteen, and Joyce and I wanted to support our mother and to support Stuart, protect his independence. There was no way we could take independent action ourselves; in those days you didn't just jump on a cheap flight to Germany and sort it out.

There was another huge complication as my father had suffered a heart attack and was probably on beta blockers, certainly on medication of some kind. My mother was being pulled every which way. She was so worried about Stuart's headaches, nausea attacks, and indigestion, but doctors she talked to wrote her off as the overprotective mother of a clearly neurotic son. Stuart was not silly about it – he went for tests, but no pathological cause was found for the headaches or stomach upsets. One doctor forcibly expressed his view that there was nothing wrong with Stuart that a good day's work wouldn't cure. Towards the end of July, however, my mother received a letter from Stuart that was evidently intended to be reassuring but in fact heightened her now permanent sense of dread. He told her he was enrolled in Paolozzi's class on a grant of a hundred Deutschmarks. He continued:

Now, as you've so often remarked (and everybody else) on how thin I am Astrids mother arranged for me to go to a very good doctor for full examination. I had X-rays many of them including Barium tests. I have gastrittis [sic], what this means is that the lining of my stomach is inflamed and swollen, also there is not enough acid in my stomach to digest my food properly, this is why I always had very bad heartburn. Now I'm on a diet of special foods, I have tablets and do exercises every morning. I must not smoke or drink alcohol etc. My appendix must come out – not immediately but in the next few months.

I have a shadow on the entrance to my lungs it is not T.B. or cancer and will be gone in a few months providing I do what the doctor tells me. My glasses were too strong and this caused me to have headaches etc. The glands in my neck are wrong this causes me to be moody and neurotic. All that is the physical side . . . over all absolutely nothing dangerous.

After electrical tests the doctor said I am a nervous wreck, in his

whole experience he has never seen anyone like me and can't believe it.
I am also under treatment for this . . . Anyway I'm in the best hands
in the world so you mustn't worry. Needless to say I am very angry
with that quack . . . remember I went to him before I came away and
told him about my trouble and all those other examinations.

. . . I'll be home in a few months or before to go into hospital to
have my appendix out. I must come home because I can't afford the
700 or 800DM.

There was also a letter from Astrid, who assured my mother
that the doctor, Peter Hommelhoff, Director of Medicine at a
Hamburg hospital and a family friend, was very good and Stuart
the perfect patient. She also said she was glad he was no longer
playing onstage: 'All morning he eat his tablets and milk-soup, he
don't smoke (only 5) and he eat only special food for his stomach.
After dinner he must sleep, and he does this without being angry!
. . . I am so happy that Stuart not play any more with the beatles. I
think this has something to do with his nerves.'

His nerves? Neither Stuart nor Astrid told my mother that Dr
Hommelhoff had indicated that Stuart's stomach problems were
aggravated by too many cigarettes, too much alcohol and Preludin.
Stuart also did not detail his blinding, debilitating headaches that
often left him gasping for breath. He was also not eating properly,
the Preludin he was taking for the pain was curbing his appetite.
He was in a terrible no-win situation. But he worked on.

Stuart kept up his studies with Scots-born Eduardo Paolozzi
between hospital appointments, and on 27 July Paolozzi wrote a
brief assessment of Stuart's progress: 'Sutcliffe is very gifted and very
intelligent, but through medical and technical reasons he has been
unable to attend for periods, which would have been beneficial for
his further development.'

Stuart wrote again saying the sedatives he was taking were
effective and he was working full days, seven and eight hours at a
time. The letters were like episodes of *Emergency Ward 10*. He had

ailments throughout his body: the medical truth seemed impossible
to find. Stuart's letters to Mother varied between 'I think I'm very
ill, I can't sleep, I can't think, I've got these crushing headaches.'
Next, she would receive a letter saying he felt fine: 'I think it's over
and don't get upset, don't fuss, don't do anything.' So she'd get all
the mixed messages, either injunctions to go and see the highest in
the land for him, which he wouldn't do, or hold off, I'm fine: don't
get too worried, don't send for me, really. She doesn't know where
she is. He asked my mother to arrange an appendectomy for him
in Liverpool in September. His upbeat tone at the start of the letter
contrasted eerily with the last paragraph, which suggested a
regression to the womb: 'Bye for now from your little boy Stuart.
Don't worry about me mummy, I'm very happy in so many ways
with my little beauty.'

My mother, understandably, was one live nerve end.

Her little boy was on his way home and we were all terribly
excited – and concerned. Especially about how he would look. My
father had suffered more heart trouble and my mother was worried
about him. She had also been in hospital for exploratory gynae-
cological surgery, so she had her own intimate concerns as well as
those about Stuart. There was a year or two where we hardly knew
from one week to the next who was going to collapse or be
hospitalized.

It was a tense atmosphere when Stuart arrived back in
Liverpool in late August 1961. We had moved to 37 Aigburth Drive,
which was in Sefton Park but had wonderful views over the
boating lake and an open-space feeling we all liked. My mother
wanted to take over Stuart's care, Astrid wanted to retain control of
Stuart's well-being. If Stuart had stayed with my mother, would he
ever go back to Germany? That was Astrid's concern. My mother's,
as always, was: if he goes back to Hamburg will he ever come
home? It was hellish for both of them. I could see how wary they
were of each other, these two women who wanted Stuart.

Their two strong personalities collided. I think the animosity that began then never went away and if anything got worse between Astrid and my mother, who saw herself as fighting for the life of her son. She was also anxious, for she had not been able to arrange an appendix operation for Stuart – the National Health wanted its own examinations before deciding that it was necessary. But, as always, she had done everything in her power for Stuart; she had arranged for our family doctor to visit Stuart at home and for him to see a consultant surgeon at Sefton General Hospital. The GP duly called at the flat, but when he reiterated his earlier opinion that there was nothing seriously wrong, Stuart asked him to leave. The consultant at Sefton General would not attempt to diagnose by using a foreign X-ray, and arranged for another to be taken; Stuart thought this a waste of time, silly and bureaucratic, and decided to hold on to his appendix and take off. On 8 September the consultant wrote in response to my mother's enquiry: 'Your son did not attend for the X-ray which I arranged but I do not think that this matters very much because the X-ray which he had in Germany was within the limits of normal, and my impression was that most of his symptoms were nervous in origin.'

Stuart and Astrid had abruptly gone back to Germany, not just because of the medical attitude but also because of the atmosphere at our house. My mother and Stuart had a row about him staying to seek further medical advice and treatment, but beneath the surface was her growing resentment of Astrid. I sensed it in the house but then did not fully comprehend what was going on. I know it was unpleasant and it must have been so difficult for them. There was Stuart looking so unwell and everyone being frustrated from all sides in their attempts to help. And Stuart not helping either by telling us what he knew we wanted to hear rather than the truth about how he felt.

When Stuart left for Hamburg my mother held on to his German X-rays and medical notes; she had the notes translated and took them with the X-rays to several people, including an old friend the dean of Liverpool University Medical School. She had tea with him and he went through all the material. He was kind but explained: her son was an artist — and she was a very involved mother. He did not tell her to get off Stuart's back and tell him to grow up, but that was the sort of message she was given.

It did not help. It was not one or the other. It eased her concerns and it did not. Stuart had never been like that before. Stuart only ever had measles in his whole life. The only childhood illness we three kids ever had in our lives was measles. We didn't have whooping cough, we didn't have anything else. Stuart was not a sick person. He wasn't a complainer. He was not neurotic about his health and so that was why it was so extraordinary. He wasn't a sickly child. He was a small child but he wasn't sickly. I can't remember a day when he was ill before that. My mother did not know what to think — what to do. She did not want to confide too much in my father in case it was stressful for his heart condition. Stuart and his letters did not help — and didn't discourage her either. His next two letters home said nothing about how he was feeling, contained no reference to his state of health. On 18 September, work was again what mattered: 'I've worked hard for the last two weeks and have quite a lot of work which I'm pleased with. I feel quite aggressive towards any critics. Soon I go to the college here to start once more. Not from the beginning but perhaps I've slipped back a bit (psychologically).'

On 6 October he reported that the clearing house at the Leicester College of Art administrative centre for graduate art-teacher training courses had supplied him with details of how to reapply for entry in September 1962. He went on:

> I am mounting the best of my work for examination by my tutor. All of it is far superior to what I would have done 1 year ago. I shall probably work 1 day (night) in the week to help out in the way of materials, I believe its quite easy for students to earn about 30DM for 3 or 4 hours work in the newspaper factories. Mind you, to work more is lunacy, particularly as its so nerve-racking and inclined to unbalance the

thought-process. I think we'll probably send more photos soon. By the way, whats the matter with Joyce and Pauline, they promised to write, I've been waiting for word from them.

Joyce was nineteen then and had been going out with the same boy for a long time, and wrote to Stuart telling him she was engaged. Her fiancé was Herman, a Belgian who at that time was working as a junior engineer with our father. So the relationship had tacit parental approval. Stuart's reaction was quite strange, as though my father didn't exist; they were projections of Stuart's own anxieties. He took on his role of family patriarch:

> *. . . you must think carefully Joyce, please, please know exactly what is important for you, exactly what marriage will mean to you, the break from your home. Love is very primitive Joyce, the cloaks and guises under which it shelters are very strange and confusing. Joyce, I felt a pang of deep pain when my mother told me you were engaged. I felt I understood the expression 'blood is thicker than water'. I was very shocked and frightened for you. Don't let Pride lead you on – or boredom!*
>
> *Think of what it's like leaving home. I feel very frightened for my mother and father in that big flat – so much money, so dangerous and insecure. Perhaps your emotions flooded up with Astrid and me because I suppose we must have represented a very romantic figure. I couldn't feel any emotion for that big place, and my mummy looked so little and helpless, she will never believe how much I understand and feel acutely and painfully for her frustration and anxieties.*
>
> *I have always been in a hurry about things, and never got to know you and Pauline very well. I'm rushing this and missing out half of what I want to say. I'll never forget when I burnt your foot with that gas poker in the bungalow . . . All that was last night, I keep forgetting what I wanted to write. That was a week ago, I don't seem to be able to get it finished so I'll post it.*

Joyce had to try to think about when Stuart burned her foot. It was long forgotten. She was the victim but had forgotten all about it: it was the perpetrator who had the conscience about an incident going back to the 1940s in our first Liverpool home. There were shades of *Crime and Punishment* even over so trivial a happening. He must have endured some hellish dreams. Stuart's worries about financial matters were over the top; my mother's health was shaky but not enough to threaten her teaching career, and although our father was close to retirement he had a pension to look forward to. And we girls would be working. I think deteriorating health had provoked much meandering in Stuart's subconscious about the need and strength of family, of close ties and love. It was there in his letter to my mother about being the 'little boy' again. When I reflect now on his mental as well as his physical health at that time it must have been such torment, such torture.

In the background was the enigmatic Eduardo Paolozzi. On 23 October 1961 he recorded without much depth of language this formal if brief assessment of Stuart's progress at college: '... Sutcliffe has become one of my best students. He is working very hard and with high intelligence.'

Stuart was still a rock and roll fan. He sent me a copy of 'My Bonnie', the record the Beatles had made with Tony Sheridan at the Friedrich Ebert Halle in Hamburg. I still have it, a collectors' dream item. Stuart was not terribly impressed about it at the time and enclosed this note with the recording. It is as written:

Here is the record that the Beatles recorded with Sheridan from the Top Ten — Its not as good as it could have been. Anyway why haven't you written to us like you promised?

Radio Luxembourg is on because Astrid is working late tonight. So lonely when she's not here. She's really wonderful and a heart of gold.

On Friday we're going to the Ballet — guess who? The 'Marquis de Cuevas' with this Russian fellow, Rudolf Nureyev, I bet you'd like that!

I've been making lithographs this week. I'm planning to paint a large painting in the next couple of weeks. Everything I've done is in the drawing line, but still good. This lithography business seems stupid,

STAATLICHE HOCHSCHULE FÜR BILDENDE KÜNSTE HAMBURG

O p i n i o n
on student STUART S U T C L I F F E
given by his Professor Eduardo PAOLOZZI:

Hamburg, July 27th, 1961

My report is, that Sutcliffe is very gifted
and very intelligent, but through medical and
technical reasons he has been unable to attend
for periods, which would have been beneficial
for his further development.

                    signed: E.Paolozzi

Hamburg, October 23rd, 1961

In the meantime, Sutcliffe has become one of
my best students. He is working very hard and
with high intelligence.

                    signed: E.Paolozzi

Für die Richtigkeit der obigen Abschrift:

Hamburg, 1-VIII-1962   (F r a n c k)
                           Regierungsamtmann

Hamburg 34 Leichenfeld 9   Behördennetz 9 - 64 - 1   Überweisungen an Landeshauptkasse Hamburg   Hamburgische Landesbank Girozentrale 50
                      Postanschlüss 25 (0 71)   Postscheck Hamburg 5000

so petty. But I don't know what the silence is, why haven't you written
at least a few words. Tell us something about the rock scene. You can tell
us a bit about the Cavern.

Anyway I'm all on edge waiting so that I can't really concentrate
to write properly. But please remind us of your existence.

I think Stuart's health was almost gone by now. He was
certainly losing it in his letters, and later he admitted in a letter to
Joyce that Astrid was losing patience with him. She was not the
Florence Nightingale he had expected, which is why his letters to
mother were more and more ingratiating. He desperately wanted
comfort – and the unconditional love only a parent can provide. He
had not mentioned his health since we had seen him in September,
but in this case no news was nothing but bad news as far as we were
concerned. My mother could concentrate on very little. Each letter
to her from Stuart brought more worry. On Guy Fawkes Night
in 1961 he wrote to us asking quite sensibly about our father's
imminent trip to Russia and went on:

I feel very much in a strange place, this college is so big, with about
four painting rooms, all occupied by very old people (not really so old),
there are many students in the place, even now I haven't been able to
assess the standard. It is high but not very original not so high as the
Slade or the Royal College. perhaps you don't know it but I'm not in
a painting class, I do general experiment under this Paolozzi fellow,
there is no a kind of criticism only a general acknowledgment of one's
presence, this is very confusing at first, even frustrating, but eventually
this becomes necessary to one's peace of mind.

I'm very much better now, not nearly so nervous or thin of course
just being here with Astrid counts for a lot. I went for a little walk to
the station for my daily papers. It's not too cold outside but in this
weather I always get headaches. I have my stipendium, 195DM in the
month, that's more than we thought and certainly more than some boys
who've been here much longer. If its possible for you to get a catalogue
from the John Moores exhibition I would be very pleased.

He wrote to me on 14 November saying Nureyev had been sensational, and added that he and Astrid were enjoying the short season of vintage Charlie Chaplin films being shown locally. He had made his own film and recorded a soundtrack for it but the tapes have disappeared. At the time he was enthusiastic, seeing the value of film to the applied arts, telling me :

Yes! Tomorrow comes Paolozzi, and Tuesday we go once more to this ship-breakers yard which we visited last semester. I will have with me a film-camera I borrowed off Theo, Astrid's cousin, I'm very quickly trying to learn the technique as I'm enthralled by the possibilities but it's so expensive.

On Saturday we were out shopping and bought material for a costume for Astrid, an orangy cord but very strong and for me a pale fawn colour for a suit which Astrid is making, will probably be finished by Christmas, she's done the trousers to trying-on stage but they'll be without pockets!!

Astrid's boss wants to buy two more pictures from me. I don't know what he wants yet but I don't contemplate letting him have them for less than 100DM each (these are drawings done in various materials on paper, some of them quite big, mostly done in the last 4 weeks) Although I can't lift the drawings and lithographs from 4 weeks work — but it's all money.

My mother hasn't replied yet but I will write in the next few days. I very much would like to know what she's thinking — My hair is quite short now almost respectable I think I must be growing up — anyway long hair definitely isn't in in Germany.

George wrote again today, and sent money for more records and said it's popular in the clubs. So you're 1 up on the others who haven't got it. Anyway Pauline, forgive me for not writing anymore, I just can't concentrate, so good night and lots of love to my mother and Joyce.

That 14 November is an important date. All the dates are. For they track Stuart's decline and the Beatles' metamorphosis into a sensational force on the music scene. Just a couple of weeks earlier

– and Hunter Davies in his authorized biography of the Beatles marks it precisely at 3 p.m. on 28 October 1961 – a young man called Raymond in a black leather jacket went into a shop in Whitechapel, Liverpool, and asked for a disc called 'My Bonnie' by the Beatles. The shop was the NEMS record store and the chap behind the counter was Brian Epstein, who did not have a clue what Raymond was talking about. He soon did. He bought in stocks of the record and as fast he got them into the shop they were sold. He was intrigued and wanted to find the source of this local best-selling sensation.

Brian, in his navy-blue cashmere overcoat and expensive suit and a Hermes navy-spotted cravat, went off to the Cavern to investigate; he must have thought he had walked into heaven when he saw the Beatles, all these butch-looking rock and rollers. By now the Beatles were in their leather bikers' jackets, and black T-shirts when they got too hot. They were generally looking Hamburg exi rather than Liverpool Teddy. Brian Epstein was so keen the groups used to call him 'Eppydemic'.

Epstein, born on 19 September 1934, was an 'older' man to the Beatles. And a sophisticated one. He had left school – one of seven fee-paying ones chosen by his parents who were a high-profile couple in the Jewish community – at sixteen and joined the family business as a furniture salesman. Two years later it was National Service but that lasted only ten months. He hated it and the army didn't care for him. He was discharged as mentally and emotionally unfit which in 1952 was the code for, among other things, saying he was homosexual. And Epstein was actively so, although homo-sexuality was illegal (until 1967, the year of Epstein's death). While stationed at barracks in London's Regent's Park he cruised the Piccadilly clubs but that landed him in trouble with the service authorities. After getting out of his 'hideous' uniform he briefly went to the Royal Academy of Dramatic Art (RADA), but an incident involving an attempt to pick up an undercover policeman in a public toilet ended his thespian ambitions. He rejoined the family business – this time selling records. It was 1957 when he started, a time, difficult to imagine decades later, when the British music industry was a comb and toilet paper affair, often a mismanagement of some trombones and washboards.

Epstein, who saw himself as the impeccable Englishman from his shiny toecaps to his bowler hat, who favoured Bach and Sibelius, insisted: 'I am not a commercial person. Really, I am a frustrated actor.' But he was a wonderful salesman. At the family furniture and music outlets – with his help there were finally nine comprising the grandest music retailer in the north-west of England – he sold records in their thousands. Later, he would try to sell Stuart a deal. Then, his customers wanted 'My Bonnie'. The meticulous Epstein finally discovered it was a German recording by Tony Sheridan and the Beat Brothers who were indeed the Beatles. Four weeks later he became the manager of what was to become the most successful group of all time.

At the same time, Stuart was inundating us with letters. He so seemed to want us in his conversations but his thoughts were more disjointed and his handwriting wilder. He wrote that, on 28 November, he and Astrid had been engaged for a year and went to a Chinese restaurant with her mother to celebrate. He said he had stopped smoking and was surprised how easy he was finding it. He also said he was disappointed he could not be back for Christmas, especially as my father would be home on leave. He told my mother: 'I hope you make him happy and he in return shows his gratification in his own charming way, which I have always loved, and you without the slightest doubt even more.' Yes, it is heartbreaking to remember. On 21 December, having enquired after the family's health, he wrote again to Mother:

> Every day has been cold this last weekly [sic], which has meant great
> discomfort etc. The little rivers had special dirty pigeons on their big broken
> ice floes – walking was very difficult. Perhaps you don't like this flat now
> as it has arrived a little – the cold, but that's always uncomfortable.

But there is no question of that, of any illness that is, I'm better than always. I am a bit fatter, perhaps you can see that from this photo. Astrid and I hope to go to Paris in April for a short while and I want to take many pictures with me to try and get an exhibition.

There is nothing intellectually stimulating here at the moment, I feel in a bit of a torpor, well and truly dumb. Paolozzi is back in England again and the rest of the class retired to the background to lick their wounds till he returns. There is only two or three of us who really work. At the moment I'm finishing off some big pieces of sculpture that I started this week. But of course I'm waiting my father's and Pauline's letters.

But we were to get our Christmas packages before Stuart got my or my father's letters. Christmas 1961 I shall never forget. Especially Christmas Day. It was when all the emotions boiled over. For us, Stuart was like Tiny Tim. We had no idea if he would survive — we didn't even know what was wrong with him. How could we, how could anybody, cure the unknown?

nine

Heaven's Door

'It was just a beginning, but there is something in Stuart
Sutcliffe that will haunt us a long time yet.'

Art critic John Willett

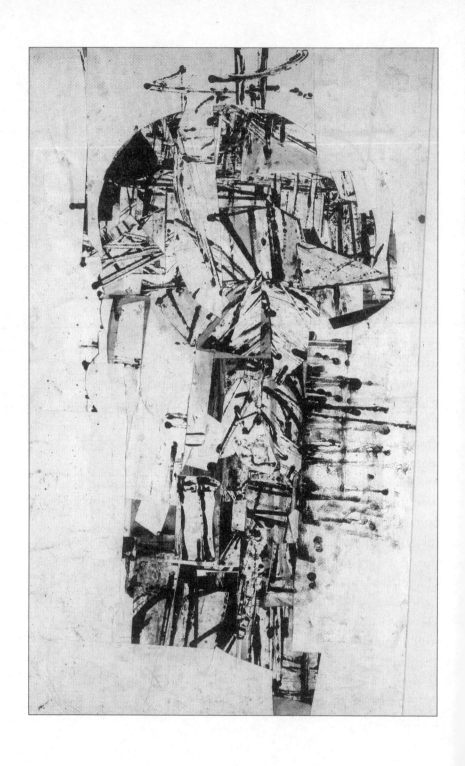

THE CHRISTMAS BEFORE Stuart died my father was home. I remember that Christmas very well because it was terribly bleak, horrible in the family. You read of extraordinary scenes, sometimes extremely violent, erupting over Christmas, for it is a particularly stressful family celebration. We tried so hard at first to make it festive for Mother, to make it traditional and joyful with a tree and trinkets; as Scots they were much more used to making a grander fuss on New Year's Eve. Such was the tension that I was, metaphorically, terrified of dropping a plate knowing that anything, no matter how trivial, could explode the situation. It's very difficult to give a very balanced picture about my father because we were his adored girls and we adored him – we had a very loving father. He and Stuart were not hostile towards one another, but my father was just absent a lot. Whenever he was home and Stuart was in Liverpool my father would go and look for him. But this Christmas, Stuart could not afford the money to come home. My father always brought presents. Our father was the bearer of gifts. He was Father Christmas all year round. The suitcase was full of stuff. From all over the place. My father took on his Santa role that year with even more kindness than usual. He required all of his serenity.

A fantastic cook, father was in the kitchen: when he was home he used to do the shopping and the cooking and I was the scullery maid. He could cook but never cleaned up as he went along, and the kitchen would be a week's work after he left it. That was another reason why we didn't let my mother near the kitchen, because she'd have gone crazy as she was so tidy. That year, she was more concerned about Stuart. She was in a terrible turmoil about my brother's health and she felt more and more frustrated. She had received nothing but mixed messages. On the one hand the medical side who had examined the X-rays and diagnostic reports were telling her that there was nothing untoward. Nevertheless, Stuart was displaying in his letters very, very worrying and frightening symptoms, yet eminent medical people were still saying there was nothing wrong. She was trying to reconcile two hugely different perceptions of what was going on. I remember that Christmas Day so well because she created such a scene.

In those glory days of public services, the postman used to deliver on Christmas Day and he brought a parcel from Stuart and Astrid. The post arrived before lunchtime. In the parcel were a brown suede handbag for my mother and a charcoal-grey roll-neck cashmere sweater for my father. There were more Dior stockings for Joyce and me. It broke my mother's heart. I've still got the gift wrap, the name tags from those gifts. It took my mother apart. It triggered something in her.

She let out the most almighty cry, a shriek. She shouted: 'My son is dying.' She shouted it again and again. She took Stuart's pictures off the wall. I went over to her and tried to hold her and called out to my father. Just as Father got to us from the kitchen my mother and I banged our heads together and collapsed on the carpet. There was blood over both our faces. I'm not much taller than my mother, and father, who was a six-footer, picked us both up and swamped us in his arms. Mother became quiet and wept and wept and my father found the source of the blood – me.

Mother said: 'Can't you see our son is dying?' At this point she realized I was hurt, but once my cut had been cleaned up and ruled nasty but not serious – I still have the small scar below my left eyebrow – Mother started again: 'No one is taking any notice. Can't you see our son is dying?'

That Christmas Day she gave us all what for as the day went on, and the what for was about nobody listening to her, nobody taking any notice of her concerns. Nobody supporting her because by now she had been to all the doctors, we're all hearing the message artistic temperament, over-concerned mother, nothing wrong with him. We were feeling attacked because it was making us feel guilty. What should we be doing? I'm seventeen. I'm eighteen in January. I don't have any money. I can't go to Germany and sniff out what's going on. So we're all backing off, trying to low key it all, and the gifts were like something cataclysmic. It absolutely broke her heart.

The Beatles were playing all-night sessions at the Cavern, and their engagement on 27 December was billed as 'The Beatles Xmas Party'. That day Stuart wrote to us, annoyed that our Christmas letters had not reached him in time: 'I haven't managed to capture any of the atmosphere at home and have no idea how things are.' On 4 January he started a letter to Mother that was enclosed with another written on 22 January:

> I got your letter yesterday so I know all is well, sorry for making you sad, but the absence of Christmas greets from you and the family was felt because of the overwhelming closeness and binding spell which Christmas has here.
>
> I returned to college today, I will start painting again next week when I have my stipendium. I really hope to stage an exhibition before the end of the year – that's for certain.
>
> Sunday. You mustn't think you are the only one I shout at! I have been liberally endowed with the Sutcliffe or Cronin temperament, whatever name it goes under, and have at times allowed it too free a hand – consequently people suffer, and often they are shocked. I don't think Astrid is completely happy. I seem to have given her the impression that she is not suitably equipped to live with me.

I'm so frustrated at my lack of equipment to deal with myself. She is so very innocent and naïve and so lovely, it's not at all fair that she must suffer – why should I have been born with such an evil weapon as my tongue. Astrid has buffeted and stood staunch and strong against any such outbursts but the threat to her poor little heart is too great, and slowly she is weakening. What can I do? Apparently nothing except wait and hope that she will continue to forgive me – but that in itself so cowardly and uncultured, is so weak.

That letter ended abruptly, with no signature. Four days later he received a letter from me and I got one back by return. This was a chatty and quite rational letter covering seven pages, the equivalent of three pages in Stuart's normal handwriting:

I haven't been out or rather 'we' haven't been out for at least a month, except shopping together on Saturday mornings. Astrid has been too tired after work and I certainly don't like going alone, but television isn't so bad, and I never fail to get the Daily Express which is by the way getting worse, particularly on its foreign policy to my mind completely unrealistic and very inhibited by conservation. On their treatment of 'the German Question', they're quite indecent.

I believe that 'Ringo' from the Hurricanes is playing now in the Top Ten with Sheridan, that's quite surprising – that news came last night along with some other news which quite excited me for a time – that is the prospect of playing bass again with a German band who lost their bass player to Sheridan. I was however completely discouraged by Astrid and her mother who were 100% against my playing. Actually it was quite unrealistic to have considered it, but for a few moments I allowed myself the luxury of being a 'rocker', I actually went along to see the band last night. unfortunately they played 6 nights a week which was much too much, That's that!

Happy birthday! Tomorrow I will try and send off some big photos for you – your express desire – and a watercolour from over 6 months ago when I started working again. Don't put it in a conspicuous position!! its only merit is its decorative value.

In his 22 January letter he seemed to belittle the disturbing nature of what he had written on 4 January. I think he would have just thrown it away if the message did not matter to him. I think of it as another cry for help, for he talked about it again. The message is inconsistent. First, he says he hasn't reread his original letter and then he quotes from it. His confusion is total.

> *I haven't bothered re-reading it as I've just laid hands on it again and would like to post something to you – I'm just on my way to college and I wish to buy stretchers as I'm painting on canvas again, I've just completed 4 big ones, 4ftx3ft, I think they're quite good, I bought quite a lot of canvas and paints last week and I'm bashing away – my stipendium was increased this month by a further 100DM. Anyway I'm feeling very happy and contented and enjoying the painting. My little Astrid is happy and contented too – I hope, it's very difficult for her, up every morning at 7.30 and home at 5.30, particularly now as she isn't interested in the creative side of the job.*
>
> *In the enclosed letter, you'll find me rather angry and bitter about my temperament but don't worry about Astrid and me, we are tied together so deeply that we can overcome it. Anyway, I don't like dramatics in letters. Has Pauline received the photographs yet? Lots of love and greetings to all.*

A few days later, Stuart suffered a convulsive fit. After treatment at the outpatients department of a local hospital, he again consulted Dr Hommelhoff, complaining of headaches and nausea. More investigations followed – blood tests, ECG (to test heart function), and an X-ray, which revealed an increase in skull pressure – but still it seemed that no definite diagnosis was possible. Astrid sent a letter to our mother: 'Stuart is very ill but the doctors say it will all be better in about 7 months . . . next month Stuart must go to hospital, his appendix must come out. . . . Our doctor was very angry when I told him about the English doktors are so stupid, and havend taken Stuarts appendix out. Sometimes Stuart is very sad, because he gets not many letters from home, but his day is so happy when you, Pauline and Joyce write to him.'

My mother was suffering internal problems and had been ill, and Joyce wrote to Stuart telling him about her having to undergo exploratory surgery. His reply, written in a very shaky hand, was brief: 'I'm so sorry that I am not in the condition to write properly. Your letter was such a shock to me, but Im also an invalid although I feel better now. I hope my mother has taken the treatment properly; but I must write to my mother I wonder if my illness is any thing to do with my mother. Anyway Joyce look after my mother and father and all my love to Pauline.'

Stuart, who was being treated with hydrotherapy and massage, came home. I think that after the Christmas crisis my father wrote to Stuart advising him of his mother's concerns and the need for her to see him. I can only guess at this but Stuart arrived home in early February 1962 to see my mother. He came on his own. My father and mother may have talked together and he might have said to her: 'Look, what can I do? I'll write to him and get him to come home and then you can see for yourself.'

Seeing him did not help any of us because he looked worse than ever. He was emaciated and his eyes were black all round. He was taking medication, drops in water. It might have been nothing. It might have been morphine. Or to get him off drugs. God knows what it was. It was only much later in life that I thought about that. As I said, I wonder how much drug-taking did go on? Astrid's mother used to get pills for them from her local chemist or doctor or somebody and that was what became, as I said, the charming story. I certainly would never rule out the impact of lifestyle on Stuart's death, but it was never the primary cause; but, of course, it wouldn't have been helpful. If you have a head injury, even quite a discreet one that's just gently leaking, haemorrhaging over a period of time, and you're taking uppers or something that puts pressure on the blood system, they would not have been helpful. Conversely, if one is in chronic pain, prescribed or not, remedies may be essential to ease the agonies, a catch-22.

He had travelled by boat and train and that had made him more tired. In those days it was about twenty-something hours. He was tired by the time he got to us. But he still wanted to go out and see John and the others. I was taken along but then taken home, as usual, before he and John and the others went out carousing.

We used to get the bus to the Cavern and did so that night. In those days if you smoked you sat upstairs. It reminded me about being on another bus in Liverpool a few years earlier. I was smoking upstairs as usual when the bus stopped; the women around me were talking about a nice young lad – 'they're not as bad as they say they are' – being 'loverly' and helping an old cripple across the road. I looked out of the window – it was Stuart assisting 'crippled' John.

It was always a lot of fun with my brother. He had black leather gloves on and when the conductor came for the money – I could see him do this with the glove – he stretched it on the hand and put it on the back of the seat in front. He placed it there as if a support for his deformed hand. He kept the conductor waiting for what felt like five minutes as he searched for the fare with the good hand. I couldn't contain my laughter. One moment we're talking about writing to our father and the next he's doing a *Dr Strangelove* act. Stuart was wearing a suit made by Astrid, fawn corduroy with very tight hips and no turn-ups, and a straight-cut collarless jacket: the forerunner of the Beatle look. It was that night at the Cavern that Paul McCartney made his comment: 'You've got your sister's suit on, Stu.'

But he would also have that style of suit on soon enough – along with John and George and Ringo Starr when he replaced Pete Best. Pete was a nice guy: fans thought him smouldering and mysterious, but he wasn't arty and I don't feel he ever had a long-term future in the band. He didn't have the same pretensions as the others. It was assumed John said: 'Get rid of Pete,' but I'm sure they were all involved in the decision. It must have been a dilemma for Brian for, according to Pete's book *Beatle!*, Brian had propositioned him.

Yet, by August 1962, Pete was out and Ringo was wearing the outfit that within eighteen months was recognized around the world as the Beatle suit. Paul's sarcasm didn't bother Stuart. He thought he looked like the bee's knees. The animosity between Paul and Stuart flagged itself again at that moment. Far more friendly to Stuart was Brian Epstein. They met at the Cavern and had dinner together. I believe John had talked to Brian about Stuart. John's conscience was still bothering him, but even without that he would have wanted to involve his friend. The Beatles were doing swimmingly, big fish in the Merseybeat pond. It was natural for John to want Stuart to be part of it. His suggestion to Brian was a compromise, one he thought would also keep Paul and George happy – and quiet. Stuart was a creative artist and it was the job of art director for the Beatles that Brian envisaged for him. But after Stuart returned to Hamburg, Brian wrote to him and in the letter that I read asked him if he would like to help him 'manage the boys'. He wrote: 'I didn't know anyone as lovely as you existed in Liverpool.' Brian said he would meet up again with Stuart in Germany and they could discuss it further – over another dinner. Even if Brian did have another agenda he was certainly serious about wanting my brother to be involved.

When John asked Stuart about his dinner with Brian and what he thought about the proposition, Stuart played for time he did not have. He said they would be in touch after he returned to Hamburg. The two said goodnight at the Cavern and John never saw Stuart again. After that visit, neither did I. I never saw him again.

As you would imagine, I have studied all the accounts of what happened to Stuart in the days before his death. I also have Stuart's letters home, which are the only real record of how he was feeling and coping. On 19 March he consulted Dr Hommelhoff after suffering another convulsive fit followed by severe headaches. Specialist treatment in a sanatorium was prescribed but — such echoes of the 2001 UK National Health Service — could not be started at once owing to a temporary lack of beds. On 29 March Stuart wrote to my mother, and I present it exactly as he did:

Sorry you've had to wait so long for a word from me but I've been ill again, I actually started a letter twice but all they contained were the phantastic hysterical wondering of a very sick little boy. If I work backwards from today healthwise I reach approximately 12 days ago, to my first moment of suffering. all in all as you might say, I'm quite a good, self-contained sufferer, I actually spoil the show by wild scream of laughter and sheer delight, the doctor comes to take my mind out of circulation — badly stated I know.

Actually I'm an acute migraine worker accompanied by my bloodlines so you can try and catch me from there. I actually hope you are not too far away from home because that might mean you're not well. God this evading the issue is killing me I'm very ill, bed-bound can't walk very far without falling over (actually I haven't told anyone, only this dressing-gown is a bit long) the same as last time, the only thing is these headaches, can't sleep, till the doc comes and injects me, meanwhile I go mad. actually I'm costing hundreds, the tablets alone. Everyone looks after me fine and chops my food into little pieces. I can't stand being ill, if it happens again I'll go berserk. 2 weeks ill, 2 weeks to recover!! god I'll never get anything done I don't know if astrid has written but she's a little queen, I've wrecked her sleep and nerves probably these last couple of weeks. Anyway forgive me for now, the incoherence and everything but its killing me writing.

My mother never saw that letter. Or any others written to her by Stuart after 29 March. I only discovered the unfinished letters when they were included in items that Astrid and Klaus Voormann put on sale at Sotheby's in London in 1985. I was sent the catalogue and that was the chance of it. I had to fight to get the letters. Tragically, that incident revealed that my poor mother died never knowing that Stuart had been writing to her only days before his death. And only later that he also wrote to Joyce begging her to get him home, to rescue him. That letter, already opened, was hand-delivered by Astrid to Joyce in the summer of 1962, three months after Stuart's death.

On 2 April, Stuart had a violent seizure. There was talk of epilepsy. Dr Hommelhoff asked for more medical opinion and two neurologists were brought in. During the tests, Stuart was asked for the first time about a blow to the head. Dr Hommelhoff talked about the vital areas of the brain — the grey matter — that are protected not by some iron casing but by delicate reefs of bone and membrane. Damage to that area from a punch or a kick to the head could be the cause of it all. The next day, Stuart began an almost illegible letter my mother never saw. I only have the following section of his message to her:

> . . . here hour after hour. from screaming at the frustration, pain and helplessness. I don't know why I can't sleep. I've had the right doses and then again, but nothing doing. I hope the concentration o this writing will tire me sufficiently.
>
> Wednesday. I suppose it will seem unfair to you, that I write only when I'm ill, but I have no alternative, the time is only 11-40 and I have been awake half an hour, I have only slept about 2 hours, most disappointing really, as I expected to be away at least until tomorrow night.
>
> I have had 4 injections since Monday and they don't half hurt. Actually I just feel drunk because I'm staggering all over the place. I've closed my eyes now, so I don't mind. or rather I hope you don't mind. I've also had a bottle of very thick beer, that is supposed to bring on sleep.
>
> It's so horrible and frustrating. 4 days without sleep, I've had all the drugs in the world. I must try and pull myself together. I must try hard. its only about 12 now, what am I to do for the other 7 hours, last night I went a walk and left the key on the inside of the door, and had to. before I could get in.

In the whole turmoil there was word of hope on 7 April. After all that happened I don't know why I am still astonished by it. The doctor said Stuart was slightly improved and comparatively free from pain. With what I know now that seems so incredible. Stuart wrote his last letter the next day. It was the one to Joyce:

still very ill . . . I'm really sad that I can't write more clearly and precisely. You know when I was lying here in bed everything seemed so easy. but I'm too soft and spoiled. Perhaps I write some more later. I want to see if I sleep. I feel so sick and stupid, and I'm evidently spoiled to death, you know. Astrid will have thousands to pay for doctors bills. In case you can't read what I wrote earlier you must find out from my father or mother if there is any epilepsy in the house (in the family I mean) Sometimes the pain is too much . . . I can't take it any more But I'm not really epileptic.

I'm at it again, I hope my mother isn't bothering as much as I am, Frau Kirchherr is ill and Astrid is worn out, I can't help it, I can't sleep . . . (this pain's killing me) They say I must come home when I am strong enough and be examined (mentally, I mean) I'm not mad as I keep saying but I know many illnesses are caused through psychological suggestion, and we can't keep this up, apart from the expense . . . I've lost 8lbs in the last 2 weeks and was definitely improving, becoming more manly, I'm terribly spoilt but I know I'm not homosexual . . . my problem seems to stem from an overwhelming self conceit and lack of respect for others, but if its not that why should I feel ill.

Dear Joyce I want you to go immediately to [the family doctor] and ask him what kind of treatment is best, You see I'll probably be better in the next few days . . . I don't care if they put me in a lunatic asylum or such a place for a couple of months – or perhaps I have electric treatment. I don't want to make out that I'm insane or something, I think its more to do with the blood, the moment I have the illness, I'm worried I've had it again 3 times. My head is compressed and filled with such unbelievable pain. I'm always sick and the pain for the moment retreats (after an hour or so) but comes back with increased vigour. At first it wasn't so bad because I didn't know what to expect, but now I can reckon on at least 8 days where the pain gets gradually smaller. If it was only once in my life I would say no more but 4 (the last 3 one on top of the other) and I must investigate . . .

Could you please make a synopsis and take it to Doctor E, and find out if its worth me coming . . . I have many X-rays from my neck. You see I'm frightened that I get it again. Perhaps Doctor E is angry with me, but if there is the slightest chance he can do anything for me . . .

Dear Joyce, I've started again, I feel a little better than before, I've got to write and explain. My illness is almost all psychological, you understand, mental, I'm not mad or anything, just not well adjusted. Today is Sunday and because she has had so much time off, she is work today.

I decided to start afresh for you. The pen is . . . but I want you to understand . . .

In early April 1962 the Beatles were a tremendously popular attraction at the Cavern and the Casbah. On 5 April they played the Cavern – it was a special appearance organized by their fan club. For nostalgia's sake they appeared first in their black leather rocker gear before changing into Beno Dorn suits and ties. The weekend of 7–8 April they appeared at the two clubs but without George, who had German measles – and they were on their way back to Germany opening at the Star Club, Grosse Freiheit, Hamburg, on 13 April. Brian did not want George to miss that opening, the start of seven weeks at the latest rock club in the city.

On Tuesday, 10 April, Stuart died. He had fainted in class, been terrified of losing his sight, had experienced such pain he had considered killing himself, but, somehow, whenever he could he painted. He worked and lived on far longer than any doctor could have expected. I think his work was the only thing that kept him going so long when he was collapsing inside his own body. The anger and frustration inside him must have been immense, been wretched. In such circumstances you try to be detached from your own life, your loves. That way it is easier to die, to leave.

Three days earlier the doctors said he could get up and paint – as long as he rested during the middle of the day. About noon on 10 April he experienced all the signs of another seizure. He was alone in the attic at Astrid's where he painted. Astrid's mother Nielsa was startled by a shout-scream. Stuart was writhing on the floor and Nielsa could not get his emergency medication into his mouth as his teeth were clamped shut. She called the emergency services but Dr Hommelhoff arrived first at 12.45 p.m. It was far worse than ever before. He called an ambulance to take Stuart to a neurological clinic. Nielsa telephoned Astrid but when she got home Stuart was in a coma. Astrid sent a telegram to my mother warning that her son was desperately ill.

The paramedics got Stuart from the downstairs bedroom and into the ambulance, but getting him to Heidbert Hospital became academic.

Astrid had his head in her hands. She said he had a smile on his face, which was nice of her. At 4.45 p.m. Stuart died on his way to hospital. His body was taken to the forensic department of the University Hospital, Eppendorf, for autopsy, which concluded that the cause of death had been cerebral haemorrhage in the right ventricle of the brain.

As soon as she could, Astrid sent another telegram to my mother with the news. It was just the beginning of her pain.

ten

We Heard the News

'I've already lost one family to produce, what?
Sergeant Pepper. I am blessed with a second chance.'

John Lennon, in a note published after his death

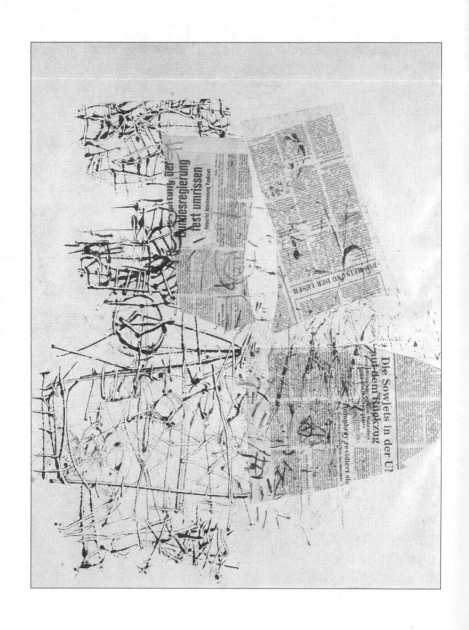

MY FATHER WAS in the middle of the Atlantic, at sea, which is how we all were when the news of Stuart's death arrived with a knock on the door. In the absurdity of death nothing was more so than the two telegrams Astrid sent to my mother. The one announcing Stuart's death arrived before the one saying he was extremely ill.

There was my mother, lost again with two different versions of events and knowing – knowing deep inside – that the worst news was the real news.

I wasn't at home when the telegrams arrived and I got a telephone message from a neighbour telling me that my brother was dead and that I needed to go home. Simple as that. No cushions to fall back on. It was such a strange piece of news to take in that I didn't know how to behave. It never occurred to me to ask somebody to give me a lift. I can remember waiting for a bus, and it was April. It was cold, it might have been raining, and I do remember feeling that I didn't care how long the bus took. Who wanted to rush back to that?

I had a fill-in job at the time, having decided not to go to art school. I worked for the Clinical Register, which was where cancer deaths were recorded, a minor research job going through hospital notes for all reported deaths of cancer. Cancer! And I was an enthusiastic smoker, so I was upstairs on the bus. I needed a cigarette – one of the few left from the packets my father had brought home at Christmas. Joyce was also on her way home. My sister at that stage was a trainee draughtswoman and later qualified as a civil engineer. She was the first woman employed in her particular office. She is a strong and supportive character. But that day the two of us were going back to face our mother who had just had the news she had dreaded for such a long time. It was a blur and thankfully so. I would never again want to see the pain that was all over my mother's face. But it was softened, if that's the word, with the determination in her eyes. I know now she planned to give Stuart a second chance. She wanted to keep him alive, and that has been my legacy too.

After the telegrams arrived my mother telephoned Astrid for more information and to make the arrangements, that dark choreography that surrounds death. I can't remember a lot of the details of that day because there was suddenly a flurry of activity to get my mother a flight to get her to Hamburg; because she was the next of kin she was the only person who could identify the body and authorize a post-mortem, which is essential throughout Europe. Stuart's death was regarded as premature, unexplained.

Allan and Beryl Williams were enormously kind and helpful, and arranged a car to take my mother to the airport. By chance, my mother was on the same flight as Brian, and George, who was leaving for Hamburg after the others because he had had German measles. I presume they must have talked and found out about Stuart, for George certainly would have wondered why my mother was on the flight.

It was Easter time so flights were busy. In both directions. Joyce and I had to arrange the funeral and for Stuart's body to be flown home; we had to make arrangements for a special lead-lined sealed coffin to transport Stuart and satisfy all the regulations. That caused more problems: we could not set a funeral date because the funeral directors anticipated that the European-style container would not fit a standard British coffin. Stuart would have smiled at the need to have a custom-made coffin. Nothing off-the-peg for him. There were flowers and guests and all the other tasks that go with grief for Joyce and me to arrange. As we all know, the worst happens afterwards. When you stop thinking about everything else – and only about what has really happened. Before my mother left we decided as a family to wait until my father had reached a port before alerting him to the news; we thought telling him by radio telephone would be too much stress on his heart.

The day after Stuart's death, John, Paul, and Pete had flown to Hamburg for their opening at the Star Club, with George, still recovering from the measles, to join them the next day with Brian Epstein. Astrid was waiting for the three Beatles at the airport and gave them the news. Pete Best reported John's reaction on being told Stuart was dead: 'John, who had been closer to Stu than Paul or me, wept like a child. I had never seen him break down in public like this before. He was absolutely shattered.' Paul also said how stricken John was: 'It really got to him a lot, he was very badly affected by it. For me it was like a distant shock at first, because we'd got used to Stu not being around. And I think I'd grown a sort of defensive shell against people dying after losing my mother at the age of fourteen. But we'd kept in touch with Stu, and when I remembered his letters had been getting wilder and wilder, I realized it must have been the symptoms of his illness and that made me feel very bad.'

They had to endure it all again when they went to meet George and Brian Epstein off their flight. Astrid was there too to meet my mother who told me that John showed no emotion at all when she arrived at Hamburg-Fuhlsbüttel airport. There was no hug, no condolences. I think John had made up his mind – he'd spent the previous night having a private wake of drink and drugs – that he was too tough to cry. That is a terrible decision to make because from then on you are living on the inside, there is no release for the pain. That way it hurts much, much more. The stories of John's insane antics in Hamburg increased from that day. He was urinating on nuns from the balcony of their Hamburg flat. He kicked a drunk in the face from the stage. He was violent, he was out of control – he was compulsive. Of course, I believe he always was. Stuart's death was another trigger or maybe, more appropriately, a launch pad for his antisocial anger. That night the Beatles were playing at the Star Club. That day my mother was agreeing that it was Stuart in the morgue, it was her son who was dead. Before leaving she agreed to the forensic pathologist's request to retain his brain for further investigations. It may still be there decades later. I don't know. But Stuart's X-rays have gone. I know my mother would have kept them – she held on to everything of Stuart's, which is why we were left with so much material – but I felt it was too morbid and destroyed them.

After that awful day of identifying her son's body, my mother spent the night at Astrid's home. My mother's relationship with Astrid had always been disrupted by their personal hopes for and needs from Stuart; it had never been good but the wound was healed for a little while and they exchanged letters almost daily. It was incredible how they developed such an intense close-ness following Stuart's death. Here were two strong woman who wanted to care for him. My mother had wanted to protect Stuart from the harm she thought was going to happen. She had not been able to do that. And, as Astrid said in her letters to my mother, *she* had lost her 'little prince'. With Stuart's death they reached out for each other. It didn't last.

My mother could never bring herself to tell us all about that night at Astrid's, and I wonder if she ever did know what happened; by that stage she must have been sleepwalking through her emotions, wandering down all sorts of corridors and banging off the walls. Who could she turn to? And she still did not know how her son had died. Sorry, she knew how he had died. She did not know why.

That night she said she went over her own life, and her thoughts focused on Stuart's Edinburgh birth and what might have happened if the family had never left Scotland. That was where the happy memories were, in Scotland. Birth and death are always times for reflection. Especially when you are about to bury a son. Mothers shouldn't bury their children.

Stuart's funeral was on 19 April 1962, Maundy Thursday, and in those days the newspapers did not publish the next day, Good Friday, to record the services. It seemed everything in our lives was awry; even the news was twenty-four hours late. It was the first day we all thought about what a short run Stuart had at life. And my mother pondered about what time of year it was and about the Resurrection. Events might have shaken her faith but not her need to keep the memory of Stuart vibrant, to keep him alive. In height, she may have been diminutive, but in resolve she had grand stature; she had her mission. I inherited it and I had to do the best with it, for it was not just for Stuart but for my mother, my father and Joyce. And myself. There is something of every enterprise which is selfish – even going to a funeral. We attend to salve our conscience about all the things we should have said and done before time ran out for any of it.

eleven

Shaken Faith

'John just can't believe that darling Stuart
never comes back.'

Astrid Kirchherr, in a letter to Millie Sutcliffe

:5:

Also I'm waiting for my suit to be
finished. black. in beautiful material.
with green lining — we were going to
have red — too bright and too unsophisticated — blue — too cold so green it is —
so — four buttons single breasted —
beautiful waistcoat with little
tiny buttons etc. trousers
without turnups (naturally)
without pockets. very tight
hips and high like a spanish

bullfighter.
the one Astrid was making for me (she
only managed to make the trousers
because work proved to much.)
is corduroy very wide ||||| in fawn
same style trousers, very beautiful

AT THE START of that Easter weekend, Stuart was buried in the Huyton parish cemetery at St Gabriel's Church where he had sung in the choir and as head choirboy had carried the processional cross. I was thinking of him in his finery doing his celestial best when his heavyweight coffin was carefully lowered into the grave. It was a much happier memory. He was interred in a suit designed by Astrid, the outfit that would become the Beatle uniform. He had written to me earlier describing the suit:'black in beautiful material – with green lining – we were going to have red – too bright and too unsophisticated – blue – too cold so green it is – so – four buttons single breasted – beautiful waistcoat with little tiny buttons etc. trousers without turnups (naturally) without pockets. very tight hips and high like a Spanish bull fighter.'

Astrid didn't come to the funeral, saying she was too ill to travel. Or Klaus Voormann. There was a vast void where the Beatles might have been. But they had just started their run at the Star Club, the very much hyped new rock venue in Hamburg. We couldn't have expected them – Stuart wouldn't have wanted them – to miss such an opportunity.

I didn't really take it in then but my mother did. All her fears had been justified. Rod Murray and Stuart's friends from art school were there. My father was en route to Buenos Aires, and it was two more weeks before he even learned of Stuart's death. George's mother attended and Mrs Harrison was lovely, helping us with tea and drinks and sandwiches back at the house. Is any funeral normal? You glide through the motions and that is what we did. We dealt with each other in a civilized way but it was the comfort of strangers. My mother had lost her world.

She resigned from teaching the day Stuart died. She never went back. She was in breach of her contract. It didn't occur to her that she could have taken some sick leave and given herself some time to recover. It was such a definite statement; she had walked away from something that she had loved all her life, teaching. I suppose her thinking was that she had lost her son, who she loved, so why not that too? Even when she was pregnant she had taken almost no time off. It was as if her life ended. Nothing else mattered. She didn't go to the Labour Party, did nothing. The education authority had to be dealt with by Joyce and me. She should have worked notice or got a doctor's certificate, but she didn't bother. She committed professional suicide. And took on the deity for good measure. She stopped going to church. How could He take these young, precious people when there is so much evil in the world? So understandable, but a difficult conflict for her. Our parish priest was marvellous. He used to come and give her Communion at home. She hadn't been to confession, so theoretically she shouldn't have been allowed it. My mother, her best friend who we called Auntie Muriel, and another friend used to go to Mass together on a Sunday. When my mother stopped attending Mass they would visit her afterwards. It was a Sunday ritual. I used to make them a little light supper before I went out, leave them talking.

Stuart and Joyce were confirmed in the Church of England and my father was High Church of Scotland; I was the one that used to go to church with my mother, so I was the Catholic with her in the family. By chance she met another priest from the past and he helped her come to some terms with the church over what had happened. With priests and Auntie Muriel helping her, she kept her faith. I don't think she ever wanted it gone, but the pain of Stuart's loss was so challenging for her to resolve. Eventually, when she started to go back to church, I used to take her and rendezvous with Auntie Muriel. The Catholic faith, the ceremony, and the warmth took her to another world and that is where, at those times, she wanted to be.

Joyce and I could see her grieving for a couple of years. She never appeared in a constant state of breakdown or crying. On the surface, she appeared normal, socially coherent. She would have visitors and would talk to John's Auntie Mimi on the phone. Outwardly, she wasn't a basket case at all. We girls would see it. She only needed to see us and she would start to cry. It wasn't until I talked to her, many, many years later, that she admitted she had a pathological fear that she would lose us too. What a terrible dread. And I also understood how much it had harmed Joyce and that she had dealt with it in her way by keeping the pain deep inside her. It was the reason I became sole executrix, for although I have always had Joyce's full support for many years she did not want to confront her loss and be that closely involved with the administration of Stuart's estate. Today, that has all changed.

I have understood more in my professional life because of what happened to my own family. It was my mother's tears that I found particularly moving. For years afterwards, she would weep when reminiscing about Stuart. I presumed that was continuing grief, but my mother did not show other signs of chronic grief. I know change occurs in the emotions of all of us following the death of someone close. My mother was shattered but survived. After Stuart's death, of course, we all had to go on living. But not the same lives.

My social life was busy and I was a regular at the Cavern, but not with any elevated status. I found the Beatles were no longer family friends. I would be at the Cavern but they would not say hello or even look at me. It was puzzling at the time but later, of course, they always cut Stuart out of any answers they gave to stories about their early beginnings in Hamburg. It was only in the 1990s that they had to start to acknowledge that he was in the band.

As a teenager, I had to deny any personal knowledge of the Beatles. Stuart had gone – what connection did I have? Almost immediately, I realized the Beatles were denying Stuart anyway and I knew that wasn't anywhere I wanted to travel. The other girls would have made fun of me if I had bragged that I knew them. Stuart's death was a spectre hovering around the success of the Beatles. It was eerie, ghostly, for I was so young – and they were too.

My mother quickly got to the thought that she would never know what killed Stuart; no one was going to say conclusively: 'This is what happened.' There was never any certainty again in her life. She continued to seek out medical opinion and have people look at the papers and the X-rays that she kept in a locked case in her room. She did get suspicious about the Beatles and vested interests – that Stuart's death would offend their image. As their careers soared even squalid old Reeperbahn, Hamburg, was a worry for them. Better not to have it on the CV. Or Stuart.

With all this feeling going on inside her, my mother was still getting letters from Astrid almost every day. After the funeral we received a letter from Astrid saying that the Beatles were being very kind and doing their best to raise her spirits, even though they too were grieving. Her first letter, as written, read:

> George's mum hath tell him all about Stuart's funeral and send the papers. I think George still can't believe it. Why can't we go for other people to heaven? John aske me that – hi said hi would go for Stuart to heaven because Stuart whas such a marvellous boy and he is nothing. hi is in a terrible mood now, he just cant' believe it that darling Stuart never comes back. I think they had a wonderful time together, and I know that John will never forget it. One day he showed me and Klaus his little room. Every piece of paper from Stuart he have stick on the wall and big photographs by his bed. Stuart darlings funny little friends miss him so much.

Astrid would tell her all about John being nice to her and

inviting her to the Star Club — but not about John saying to her: 'Stop sitting at home — it won't bring Stu back.' I was told years later when I talked to Jurgen Vollmer. Astrid's letters also talked of John being devastated which, with all we know now, he would have been and enormously so. Through these letters an intense relationship was created between Astrid and my mother. Then my mother noted that Astrid would write about the Star Club and her nights out there. She also wrote a great deal about how kind George was being to her, buying her a leather coat for her birthday, and so on. This began to needle my mother and contributed to the breakdown in their relationship.

I did not see Astrid for thirty-two years after she visited home in 1962. John visited us one evening in 1963, and Paul agreed to my interview with him. But George, mother's favourite, we never heard from again. Astrid photographed many British groups, including the Searchers, who followed the Hamburg rainbow in the aftermath of Stuart's death. Hamburg, of course, had been the Beatles' springboard to fame and many others chased that pot of gold. Astrid was the German connection with the Beatles. One of the Merseyside groups which played in Hamburg was the Undertakers, and Jackie Lomax played the bass and sang. They played in Hamburg for nine weeks in the summer of 1962 and Jackie and Astrid were said to be very close. Certainly, later that year the story of the two of them rattled all around the Cavern. Astrid was also still very much involved with the Beatles, now very famous, and worked with them as a photographer on several projects. Astrid was getting on with her life and understandably so, but it made my mother wonder. Just how much had she loved Stuart? What had it all been about?

The break-up between Astrid and my mother was inevitable and, of course, it was about Stuart. Or, rather, his possessions. My mother wanted Stuart's paintings, letters and other effects that were at Astrid's home. Astrid had written to my mother saying that when she felt better she would put Stuart's things together and send them to her. In her letter dated 30 May 1962 she said that she kept Stuart's photograph by her bed with a fresh flower. She said Stuart looked like a little prince. She also apologized for 'making' more photographs for my mother and added: 'As soon as I work again I will make them and I will send darlings' [sic] things to you as soon as I feel well again.' More than a year later nothing had arrived. My mother wrote asking the return of Stuart's things. That was when the bust-up between them took off. In 1963, Astrid was in Liverpool working as a photographer with the Beatles but we never heard from her. We saw photographs of her at Mrs Harrison's house. Still, none of Stuart's belongings had arrived. My mother felt that not only had her son been forgotten but that his things did not matter either.

The loyalty dispute and battle over Stuart's legacy began. Astrid and my mother's falling out over it was venomous. Such an intense emotional union between two individualistic women erupted in a volcano of acrimony. It was brought home to me how cruelly the relationship had deteriorated when I saw a letter from George reproduced in *Hamburg Days* in 2000. He and the other Beatles were staying at the Palace Court Hotel in Bournemouth, in August 1963, when he sent Astrid a letter asking if he could have and use some of her photographs of the Beatles. He said that John and Paul were going to make money from their songs so he wanted some unseen photographs for a book. He and Astrid had obviously been talking about my mother and all that had happened to Stuart. Astrid, I can only presume, had complained about my mother to George, for he wrote on the hotel newspaper: 'I know you are very particular about what you do with all your lovely photos, but if you are nice and send me some with the negatives, then I will kill Mrs Sutcliffe for you! But if you don't, then I will pay for Mrs Sutcliffe to go to Hamburg and see you for a Holiday!!!' George was obviously not serious and was still a young man when he wrote the letter, so did not appreciate the depth of feeling involved. But I would have thought that all these years later he would have been more careful about allowing such a letter to be published. For nearly four decades after Stuart's death, it hurt even more to see it.

At the time, my mother found some calming comfort from Rod Murray and his first wife, who were so kind to her. They used to invite her for dinner and take her out and gossip to her, try to keep her going. It was hard work but they persevered magnificently. Finally, some months later, a crate of Stuart's things arrived. We ticked off the items from Astrid's inventory and there were the paintings, sketches and notebooks, and Stuart's clothes which my mother gave away to needy families.

And the Beatles were a success. The very first airing on radio of 'Love Me Do' I remember very well indeed. It was on very late at night in October 1962, and we'd been alerted in *Mersey Beat* magazine and the local papers that it was going to be on. I'd just had a bath and mother, Joyce and I sat around the wireless to hear it. There had been such a fuss locally. I had such mixed feelings about it. I thought it was excellent and I was excited, and the other part of me was crushed with all the memories of Stuart and these boys. It might have been easier if I'd hated their music but I didn't. Parlophone, an EMI subsidiary, had signed the Beatles not long before Ringo Starr replaced Pete Best on the drums. Beatlemania was soaring. The phenomenon of these four sinless (according to the *Sunday Times*) boys had started. But when 'Love Me Do' was released the Beatles were still playing at lunchtime at the Cavern.

Within a year they were overshadowing the Great Train Robbery, and the John Profumo affair and Christine Keeler. The Beatles were the soundtrack to such events, to much of the sixties. And, indeed, to a great many people's lives yesterday and today, with their 2000 compilation of number-one hits itself being a number one in thirty-four countries. No one could ever deny their impact on our world – which for me, of course, makes even more strange the way they chose to forget Stuart.

My mother's world revolved around Stuart. The more successful the Beatles became, the more she wanted Stuart's artistic work to be recognized – acknowledged, but apart from his association with them. That was always going to be difficult for her, because at that time he did not have a reputation as an artist. My mother would get angry when her attempts to get exhibitions of Stuart's work organized met with obstacles. The art historian and critic John Willett was always helpful, but he told us that he met great opposition to a show in London. It is clear that approaches were made to the Beatles about such shows that my mother knew nothing about it. It was not about asking their permission, but some enterprising types wanted their endorsement to exploit Stuart's Beatles connection rather than his artistic work. Yet that was the last thing my mother wanted. If anyone got near enough to ask any of the Beatles they'd say no. If any connection with the Beatles was mentioned, those involved were dismissed as opportunists. But it was the only hook the media had – and that would backfire on her, for it would look as if she was using it. It was quite a nightmare.

She had such an utter belief in Stuart's art, and had been encouraged in that by notable artists and critics. She had subscribed to the belief that an artist's work should and does live on, but by doing so brought scorn and accusations of opportunism. Once again she was caught on the horns of a dilemma.

In May 1964 a major memorial exhibition for Stuart was held at the Walker Art Gallery in Liverpool where he had sold *Summer Painting* for the £65 that bought the blonde. Stuart's former tutor Nicholas Horsfield, John Willett and deputy director John Jacob, helped select the works to be exhibited and there was national publicity. That interest told my mother that Stuart was not going to be an artist in his own right, but that he was the early Beatle. The one that died. She had the growing realization that we would never get out from underneath that. Stuart's show was a great success, attracting more crowds than any other one-man exhibition, more than ten thousand people in the three weeks his work was displayed. The Beatles, of course, were attracting even larger numbers.

They had appeared at a Christmas show at the Empire Theatre

in Liverpool on 22 December 1963, and returned there on 8 November 1964. It was a homecoming of heroes, international idols with eleven chart singles, three albums, the film *A Hard Day's Night,* and a major American tour. It was an enormous event, and fanfares everywhere you looked. Shortly afterwards, John came round to visit my mother. He was off to Sheffield the next night and to Bristol the day after for the end of their triumphant UK tour. Bill Harry, who was editing *Mersey Beat*, had kept in touch with my mother and when he saw the Beatles that night he asked John if he would like to go and visit Stuart's family. John instantly thought it was a good idea. He and Bill and Pete Shotton, who was in the Quarrymen with John, went round to Aigburth Drive in John's Rolls-Royce and my mother was delighted to see them. She fussed over them. John was so different to us. He was tender, affectionate. He kissed me and my mother. He swept me up in his arms and was so tender and loving. That was the other side of John. He was living with Cynthia and Julian in Weybridge, in a large house with six bedrooms and secluded grounds. He was the successful rock star then and apparently very happy. Certainly, he was that night – and so different from that incoherent hybrid character we had met with Stuart not that long before. We talked about Stuart and the art school days and painting and so on. John was a delight and my mother was delighted. It was like the old days for us, the days when Stuart was there too.

Mother had what I suppose was a shrine to Stuart: examples of his work all around the flat, on the walls and even under some beds. Her passionate interest was promoting Stuart's work. My mother, seeing John, remembered she had a book he had lent to Stuart, *How To Draw Horses*. John had won it as a prize at primary school. She went off to find it for him and told the two visitors to choose something of Stuart's to take as a remembrance. Bill picked a huge collage of Stuart's. My mother brought back a newspaper cutting for John, the Beatles' first review from June 1960. She asked him to take something of Stuart's for himself and he chose a long, black scarf that Astrid had knitted. As an art piece, with my mother telling him to take anything he wanted, he picked a wonderful blue abstract. It would, he promised, take pride of place on his wall.

We never saw John again. Or the blue abstract. It has disappeared. John left us in his Rolls with the abstract and that was it. Later, he said it never left him but Cynthia told me she had never seen it in her life. She was quite amazed and she said: 'If John had walked in with a Stuart Sutcliffe you'd know that through thick or thin I would have looked after that picture.' I thought it must be in America with Yoko Ono. In 2001, Yoko was contacted by the organizers of Stuart's Rock and Roll Hall of Fame exhibition but wrote back saying she knew nothing of the blue abstract. I could get paranoid about its whereabouts, but who is to know? When I talked to Cynthia in 2001 she had no idea that John had been round to see us that night after the Liverpool Empire show. There were lots of things going on that not everybody knew about.

Not too long after John's visit his Auntie Mimi came to visit my mother. They were like dogs sniffing out each other but they knew how close Stuart and John had been. In a way, they had both lost their boys and, from that meeting, they were constantly in touch. John did not often contact Mimi and when he did it was superficial information that she got. I was aware of news of John through my mother but it was low on detail. The Beatles had left Liverpool, though not our lives, for there was always something there to remind and involve us.

twelve

The Price of Life

'You didn't go on holiday with queers or else you bloody were one.'

Paul McCartney on John Lennon and Brian Epstein

Thursday

Dear Dad.

Perhaps you aren't at home when this gets there but this is something for your birthday from Astrid and sorry me. Its late, but better late than never. You must write to me, and please forgive me not writing buts its very difficult to follow your movements. I hope you are well

your loving son stoat

XXXX

MY MOTHER RETURNED to the family when my father died. That was when he was home in 1966. He was talking about retiring from the sea and enjoying life, pottering about and meeting friends for a drink and long talks.

Brian Epstein, who had founded NEMS Enterprises in June, 1962, had become a serious conglomerate in the popular music world of the sixties with a stable of stars, including Cilla Black. When he died, a year after my father, he was holding Cilla's first BBC contract in his hands. Brian's father had died six weeks earlier. Brian's mother, Queenie, reached out to my mother for help.

They were heartbreaking times. I was 20 when my father died. He was 60. He certainly had some style in the way he choreographed his departure. He was back from a trip and as usual messing around with a crony, a journalist called Don Smith who did theatre reviews for one of the red-top newspapers. Sometimes they would go to the theatre together and in the interval they would write the review and phone it through. Don had taken my father to a press launch over the water, under the Mersey tunnel, at a car factory. I received a phone call from a hospital: 'Your father has had a major heart attack, he is insisting on going home. It is against medical advice. You need to get your mother home.'

Joyce had married and given birth to her first child. It was a boy, David, and what a joy. The circle of life, especially for my mother who had another boy to dote on. And that day that's where my mother was – with her grandson. Father told the doctors my mother was at Joyce's house, which was a forty-minute drive from us. I was told to get our GP to be present for father's return. He had signed himself out. They couldn't keep him in hospital against his wishes. He would not come home in an ambulance and instead arrived in Don's car. He *and* Don, who my mother couldn't stand, came in. There were quite a few steps up to our front door – and father strode up them having just suffered a major heart attack.

He was fully clothed, tie neatly knotted as always, climbing up these steps as if nothing had happened, and came into the sitting room. I looked at them and he asked me to get drinks for him and Don. I asked: 'Daddy, is this wise? Well, at least sit down. Mother's on her way and so is your GP and he expects to see you in your pyjamas and in your bed.' He said: 'Oh, Don's just staying for a drink.'

And so everybody arrived: the doctor, my sister, and my mother, who was furious with anxiety and distress and goodness knows what else. But there were father and Don, sitting and drinking whisky. My mother, who did not often panic, was flapping and hugely upset with Don who she thought should at least have had the sensitivity to leave or at least say: 'Come on, Charles, let's get you to bed.' I was sent in to my father because I was the one he took notice of and I did the 'Come on Don you'd better get off' act. We got rid of Don and my mother got father to bed. Meanwhile, the GP was waiting all this time to do a further examination and go through the medication.

The rehabilitation process is that after so many days you have to get up, put on your dressing gown, and walk around. He was doing very well indeed. He had been told to have one drink a day and no cigarettes. He never touched a cigarette or a drink again, which may have helped kill him because he probably should have had at least one drink to thin the blood. He was making very good progress. His hairdresser would come to the house. It amuses me now to think he had facilities that men today regard as luxuries. The hairdresser would come and do his eyebrows and moustache and trim his hair and shave him. He was recovering very nicely. And with some of that very Scottish, charming Charles Sutcliffe style.

Don would come to visit but even that didn't tempt my father to drink or smoke. When he was home he would always make our breakfast but after his heart attack that naturally did not happen. Yet, on the day he died, 18 March 1966, he got up and made me a breakfast of eggs and bacon and toast. He took tea and the newspaper, the *Daily Express*, to my mother. He kissed me goodbye and saw me off to work and went back to bed, next to my mother, and had a huge heart attack. He died three weeks to the day he had walked in from hospital. My mother telephoned me at work and Joyce and I arrived at the house about the same time.

It's quite a remarkable thing to say, but in a way my father's death made my mother. It was like it jolted her into caring for us. She looked after my sister and me as if father's going was our death, our exclusive hurt. It was hers as well but when my brother died it hadn't really occurred to her that we were in grief as well. It wasn't just a mother and father who had lost their boy, we'd lost our brother.

My father's death transformed all of that for us, for my sister and me, for my mother took charge, looked after us, looked after everything. All the things she didn't do for Stuart she did for my father. She made all the arrangements for the funeral, for my father to be buried next to Stuart. My father had prepared for his death. He had absolutely everything ready. Everything. All his papers. Everything was in order. He'd done it during that three weeks. All was available for mother.

I was chivvying him when he got back from the hospital that first day. I said: 'It's foolhardy. You need to be in intensive care. There could be another clot running around—' He interrupted me: 'If I'm going to die darling, I'm going to die in my own bed.' And he did.

Tragically, Joyce lost a child that had gone full term after father's death. My mother was strong. Within a year she started doing temporary teaching jobs, filling in at schools that had somebody on sick leave so that she didn't have to make a commitment. A term here and there was what she started to do. And it gave her some purpose. As well as keeping an interest alive in Stuart's art. Between 1965 and 1967 she staged, with the help of Nicholas Horsfield, three more exhibitions of Stuart's work in Liverpool. In 1967, some of his work was included in an exhibition at the Institute of Contemporary Art in London that was staged to run alongside the publication of John Willett's book on Liverpool artists, *Art in the City*.

That year Stuart appeared on the album cover of the Beatles' landmark recording, *Sergeant Pepper's Lonely Hearts Club Band*. If you look at that cover he is on the top right-hand corner and it is very difficult to see who he is. We all now know, historically, that nothing ever got done unless all four of them, Paul, George, Ringo, and John (and now John's estate), agreed. I was told that John insisted that Stuart went on the *Sergeant Pepper* cover – somewhere. But it is so discreet. When the sleeve is used as an iconic photograph it is usually cropped so that Stuart is cut off.

The year of *Sergeant Pepper* was also the year Brian Epstein died and his mother and mine would be united in grief. After Stuart's death, our family life was radically changed. What of Queenie, who had lost her husband and a son within weeks? After Stuart and my father, I think that my mother and I did our best to resume our lives and tried to hide our grief from one another. My mother seemed to lose her zest for life and the house seemed sad and empty. But that was helped by the visits, which would always involve tears, that Auntie Mimi and Queenie made to my mother; I was always touched by the concern and affection they showed. They had met in the very early days of the Beatles and stayed firm friends. The three women were linked by the Beatles and by tragedy; first Stuart, then Brian and, later, John.

Brian was enduring long bouts of depression and haphazardly drifting along in his own perilous ocean of drink and drugs, delusion and disillusion. His lifestyle was wanton and there would be country-house parties where anything went. The Beatles had stopped touring in 1966, and Brian's hold over them had all but evaporated. They did not seek out his guidance and help. Why should they? Brian had 'lost', in stupid investments, at least a million pounds of their money – and that was a huge sum all those years ago.

On 27 August 1967, after a bank holiday weekend, Brian was discovered dead at his home in London's Belgravia. Rumours and theories spread with the big headline news of Epstein's early death exactly three weeks before his thirty-third birthday: he was the victim of the rough homosexual sex he favoured; a lover had murdered him; a burglary had gone wrong; he had committed suicide – something he had attempted before. The speculation was mixed in with facts. Epstein's father Harry, until 1966 a warden at the Greenbank Drive Synagogue in Liverpool, had died only five weeks earlier. Epstein had sat *shiva* (traditional Jewish mourning) for his father and was terribly concerned for Queenie's welfare – and for his own health, having just left a private clinic. And the Beatles' contracts were about to be renegotiated at the end of September. Epstein had much on his wandering, often drug-befuddled, mind. There were empty pill bottles around. I suspect guilt at losing the money was uppermost in his mind, and having just lost his father. Terrible turmoil. 'He was one of us,' said John Lennon. But when Brian died he wasn't really. Things were starting to fall apart for Brian. He'd sort of lost the Beatles, who were some of the world's most powerful people.

Almost everyone who encountered Brian in the sixties found him a kind, tolerant man. I met him several times with Stuart at the Cavern and at his offices. He was always polite and well-mannered. There are scores of recorded examples of his benevolence to others, often helping out with cash to singers or acts who had stumbled at music-business hurdles. Before his death, Brian was using more and more drugs to get to sleep. And when he did close his eyes and drift into an uneasy rest he would often sleepwalk. Then, he would snap awake and work on his papers, on contracts and schedules for his growing roster of acts. His need to do well by the stars he had helped create was what kept him going. There were plenty of them. In 1967 he had seventeen acts and composers, from Henry Mancini to Gerry and the Pacemakers, folk singer Donovan, crooner Matt Monroe, the Fourmost and Billy J. Kramer and the Dakotas. Along the way he also represented the first *British* bullfighter, Henry Higgins, who fought under the name Enrique Canadas.

But Brian's huge status came from being the man who signed the Beatles. Others may have rated them but it was Brian who put them under contract and so successfully launched them. People, in and out of the business, simply accepted that they were Brian's creation. He must have been so hurt by John's bitter words about being turned, by Brian, into sanitized, floppy-haired idols from the original leather boys image. And John's statement; 'I suppose there was that kind of homosexual thing'.

In Liverpool – all over Britain – there was no such thing as 'gay' gossip. Homosexuals were 'queers' and the law supported that general verbal verdict. To the Beatles and British 'beats' in those very early sixties 'being queer' was a bit of a joke. They had no understanding of the anguish that Brian and others suffered because of the law and public opinion. Even the supposedly 'with it' and turned-on Beatles were not truly aware of the homosexual world. Paul McCartney said that he heard about 'gayness' from Royston Ellis. When I interviewed him for the book he talked about John and Brian's Spanish holiday: 'The rumours about Brian and John were caused by John going on holiday with him. No one did that, you didn't go on holiday with queers or else you bloody were one. From where we came from that was the attitude but John was more—' He broke off there and then went on about Stuart and John:

'A rumour? I don't know. That question is very strange, fraught with danger. I basically say to people: "Well, none of them made a pass at me." I don't know if it's true but you must have been bloody damn good at fooling people – we were in bloody hotel rooms with them. I saw them pissed out of their skulls. Anyway, who cares? I don't. I am secure in what I am, in my sexuality.'

In the mid-sixties the Beatles were running the world. I think about how young these guys were when they had such spectacular, mega success. They were not fully formed as personalities, for they had only lived for twenty-something years. They were not mature people. The parameters hardly extended beyond how much money they would make and how successful they would be. And very quickly came all the entourage, all the support systems. The days of squalor in Hamburg were over – they went from that to the other extreme, which was luxury beyond anything they could ever have thought of; they had lavish estates, and fleets of people who were just gofers. If a Beatle said 'I want,' well, somebody went and got it.

For years they had been hoofing around the dance hall circuit and back to Hamburg; they didn't have a fixed life. They didn't go to the Co-op did they? They didn't help. Even when John and Cynthia were together, even when Julian was born, John wasn't having to think about how they were coping. Could Cynthia do the washing, ironing and raise the baby? It didn't matter, for all he had to do was get someone to fix it. They never experienced the responsibilities of growing up in real life – they never had to do it. When George wrote that letter to Astrid asking for some of her photographs to use in a book, he is certain he can do anything he wants. It's not: 'God, I would dearly love to do a book and I wonder if I will ever be lucky enough to find a publisher.' It's full of assumptions. They can do anything they want. And that was always their attitude to our family. They wanted to keep Stuart shut out, and as much as my mother tried to promote Stuart's paintings without the Beatles link, the more others introduced it and they fought it. Why? Was there any need to deny Stuart's contributions, especially after they were so established around the world? By then any of the Musketeer element of the Hamburg days had vaporized.

After Brian's death, it all seemed to get into a mess for the Beatles although, initially, it did not appear that way from outside the circle. The feuds between them, with Paul in one camp and John, George, and Ringo in the other, were all about personal, business, and musical differences, according to Paul. But they were hushed up for a myriad of legal, commercial and image reasons. What the world saw in the late sixties was the most popular band of all time with fabulous international success, favourable box office films, and, of course, multimillion-selling records. If anything, they were even more popular in America and Japan than in Britain. The Beatles ruled the world but not, it seems, themselves.

Cynthia had found John and Yoko, who had moved in with her belongings, having breakfast together when she returned to their home in Weybridge from a trip to Italy, and that effectively was the end of the marriage and life at Kenwood, St George's Hill. The break-up between John and Cynthia and the emergence of Yoko as his girlfriend and then wife – they married in Gibraltar in 1969 – was interpreted by many as what ended the Beatles. It doesn't seem that way to me. The boys were arguing before Yoko appeared, but she aggravated the situation: her influence over John and her appearance at their recording sessions marked her out, for them, as an intruder. John and Yoko were living at Tittinghurst Park, where John recorded 'Imagine' on his Steinway piano, and her influence was pervasive. Even more so, I would presume, in the perception of Paul and George and Ringo than it actually was. John was certainly protective of his relationship with Yoko and was upset that friends and the other Beatles would, in his view, 'shit on' it. John, in a letter to Paul McCartney which was being auctioned at Christie's in London in late 2001, reacted to an admonishment from Linda McCartney about remarks he had made about the Beatles. It was written almost a decade after Stuart's death but included in the six handwritten pages, filled with cursing and crossings out, was a reference to our mother. I can only guess that Paul had mentioned

Linda's comments to John in an earlier letter for John replies 'I was reading your letter and wondering what middle-aged, cranky Beatles fan it was who wrote it. I kept thinking who it was: Queenie? Stuart's mother? . . . What the hell, it's Linda!' John wrote the letter when the Beatles were tearing themselves apart and he was brutal to Paul about what he thought the effect of fame had been on him: 'Do you really think most of today's art came about because of the Beatles? I don't believe you are that insane. Didn't we always say we were part of a movement, not all of it? . . . Get off your gold disc and fly.' The letter was being sold by an anonymous person who had bought it in an American auction in the early 1990s. A Christie's spokesperson was quoted as calling it a 'historical document' and added: 'It's the two key Beatles and epitomises their relationship during this bitter feud.' For me, it is just another example of how complex it all was for them and all the more so with Yoko in John's life; that meant Yoko was a remarkable, intriguing presence in all their lives.

In the mid-1960s a consciousness was being raised with regard to women's politics. Yoko was involved in that movement with other high-profile women in America who were then called feminists. Her philosophy as an artist was that she was part of the fluxist movement that included other performing artists. I would put the fluxist movement to the left of the surrealists. This was the combination Yoko brought to her relationship with John. John appeared satiated with his life so far, and Yoko was a bolt out of the blue. She stretched everybody's credulity – was she daft, a con artist or an original? John had never closely encountered a woman like this before. The nearest to it would have been Stuart but he was male so it was OK to be together. But there was a similar dependency. Yoko, like Stuart, could validate John's other side, his intellect, his tenderness. I think Yoko energized John intellectually and emotionally. In John's attempt to embrace this 'new woman' and become a 'new man' he seemed to be like all converts – too serious, too naïve.

Of course, it did not help either them or their cause that they were often drug assisted which made them appear at times, at the very least, incoherent. I think this clouded the waters of what I believed was an important matter.

I can imagine the shock to the other Beatles' systems having to accommodate another person in their group; the whole dynamic was upset. They must have been amazed to witness John deferring to and being inclusive with a woman. These boys were used to deferential shadows in the background. John's natural inclination was to lead and so, to those looking in, Yoko often looked intrusive or pushy if she tried to express her views. The struggle between them to be equal often had the adverse effect of messing up the message. At highly public events this often left them exposed and vulnerable and open to ridicule. Yoko usually got the blame.

John was no longer the witty, cocky individual. I think Yoko liberated John rather than breaking up the Beatles. John gave Yoko a world stage to advocate the beliefs she held before she met him. I think Yoko was ahead of her time in that world of rock and roll but not in the intellectual fringes. What resulted was John's difficulties with *power sharing* – who was the boss? – and there was an imbalance. Yoko became dominant, and that wiped out what they had started out to achieve – equality. It was another example of John's obsessiveness and his dependency. I think this, and John's break-up with the Beatles and Cynthia and Julian, which may have led to disappointment, disenchantment, loss of self in John, and which manifested itself in the power struggle between him and Yoko. A struggle to retain the integrity of their personalities. The John and Yoko affair, which began as liberation, became imprisoning for John. Which was what John's flight to Los Angeles with May Pang was all about: he fled his prison. His 'long weekend' away turned into a year.

I think he went looking for his freedom, independence, and himself. Instead, he lost himself further in drugs and drink and violence. His relationship with May Pang was the old-fashioned kind, the traditional kind as in the past. Only a year after John and Yoko moved permanently to New York, with John never returning to Britain, he took off for Los Angeles with May Pang who was his secretary, which as I suggested earlier was another symptom of his compulsion. They were together for more than a year, most of which John spent in chemically enhanced disorientation. Could it be that the divorce he had demanded from the Beatles, like the one from Cynthia, was too much for him to cope with? And then he abandoned May Pang as he had Cynthia and Julian, back to his old pattern. There were no thoughts for others. When he returned to Yoko there was a new hierarchy: she was the one to do the business and he was the house parent to Sean.

Yoko was the one who flourished: she was off drugs and took on John's role, protecting and fighting for his rights. The much-written-about Lennon Diaries may have included drug-fuelled fantasies rather than accurate recordings of real events. However, they suggest that he was not happy in his new role. At the time of his death the rumours in the circle around the Beatles was that John was returning to Britain and leaving Yoko. Yoko has maintained ever since John's death that they were a very deeply loving, together couple. Perhaps they found an accommodation in their separateness: John the obsessive recluse, Yoko the successful business-woman.

In the interviews carried out with them in the last few months of John's life, they appeared intelligent, articulate, coherent, and had a good rapport and balance. They were sharing equally. They also had reflectiveness, which is a very important quality for people to have. The politics were the same but sharp and focused. They were also back in the recording studio, and I wondered if the John we knew had grown up and matured. Had he found happiness and contentment? Or was he wracked with guilt and remorse and still fighting his demons? These are the conundrums and we will never truly know the answers.

Of course, for me Yoko provoked all the echoes of the past, of Stuart and John. How Stuart was the one who was between John and Paul. We must all bring our own interpretations of what jealousies or fears did really lead to the abandonment of the Beatles. I would suggest that it had to do as much with personal relationships and power as with artistic ambition and financial awareness.

I know how Stuart was treated as John's close friend, and because of that I must have some sympathy for Yoko. When Liverpool University presented her with an honorary degree on 2 July 2001, I was invited as one of her special guests. It gave me goose-bumps to watch Ms Yoko Ono Lennon, who looked so tiny in her cap and gown, getting her honour from the university's Faculty of Engineering. This was the woman who had joined John in his rebellion now accepting a traditional degree in his home town. At the same time my heart went out to Cynthia who was discarded so easily by John. John had decided – in an instant – that he was moving home to live with Yoko and leaving Cynthia and Julian. Like a click of his fingers, it just happened. Of his relationship with Yoko, John offered the classic: 'It's just handy to fuck your best friend.'

The disentanglement of the Beatles was more complex and crazy than even the worst domestic dispute. They had created their company Apple in 1967, a brand name much like Richard Branson did with Virgin, spinning off from popular music into all aspects of business to run on very high-minded lines. Unlike Branson's empire, this one was a financial sieve which became more and more complicated; John and Yoko signed up Allen Klein to sort it out. The appointment of the American accountant had the support of George and Ringo. The snag was Paul. He had fallen in love with Linda Eastman, soon to be his beloved wife. He wanted her father Lee Eastman, a revered attorney in New York, to clean up the Beatles' business affairs. It was acrimony ever after. John was famously quoted as saying he wanted to separate from the other three and telling them: 'I want a divorce – just like I had from Cynthia.'

On 10 April 1970 fans around the world heard that the Beatles were effectively no more. Paul had made that positively clear in an interview released with his album *McCartney*. That news shunted everything else down the day's television and radio news bulletins and newspaper front pages. The next month the Beatles' album *Let It Be* was released; it had begun life a year earlier as *Get Back*, and provoked more argument over its production values and marketing.

I remember seeing a London *Evening News* newspaper on New Year's Eve 1970, and the main story was about Paul suing the others in the High Court. He wanted to wind up their deal, their partnership. Paul wanted to get out of Apple, and to do that he had to bring a legal action against John, George, and Ringo. It went on for a long, long time. That twinkle, the fun and enjoyment in their talent that had been so much of their success, had vanished into a different world. Flower power dissipated them. Albeit arrogant and cheeky, full of marijuana and meditation and Maharishi Mahesh Yogi teachings, they were never to be the same young boys I had seen so often at the Cavern or at our house. Or to stay very long together in their New Age manifestation. The Apple debacle saw to that, with all sorts of legal developments and upsets between them. It was in August 1971 that Paul wrote his 'Dear People' letter, saying it was time for him to withdraw from the Beatles fan club. Given the horror around the world at the break-up of the group it began, for me, amusingly:

As you may know, the band split up a year ago and has not played together since. Each of us is getting together his own career, and for this reason, I don't want to be involved with anything that continues the illusion that there is such a thing as the Beatles.

Those days are over. In the past you have been great supporters, and the idea of this letter is to let you know how I want it to be in the future, in case you wanted to know. Now I'm not a Beatle any longer, and want to get back to where I once belonged — living my own life, having my own family, my privacy, and getting on with my music.

John had started painting seriously in the early 1970s and his work was remarkably like Stuart's. Well, it would be: Stuart had helped teach him. He did large abstracts using palette knives rather than brushes to apply the paint. Later, Paul took up oil painting. Paul told me: 'I used to think I was a better drawer than John. If we had a person to draw I got a really good likeness and to me that was what drawing was about. Now, that's not necessarily so. I've learned that it's to do with other things as well. I remember John trying and in my little mind I thought: "Well, I can do it. He tried and he went to art school and he didn't get a very good likeness." I always had faith in what I did but because of the ethic "you didn't go to art school" I didn't get into painting until I was about forty and I started painting anyway and felt at ease with it, no torment. I had a friend visit and look at my work and she said: "Paul, I wonder what a psychiatrist would make of these?"'

Stuart's work, through my mother's efforts, was on display regularly in Liverpool and there were exhibitions in other parts of the country and abroad. She received much high-level support. Sir Kenneth Clark, later Lord Clark, who through television was a high-profile art critic and historian, complained in a letter to her about opposition to greater exhibitions: 'What is wrong with our world? Your son was so obviously gifted and anxious to be true to his feelings. I feel mad in sympathy — there are times when the miserable confusion of the modern world drives me to despair. But one must resist it.'

I had left home to pursue my career and first I did my A levels in London. I went home about every other weekend — and I did my own laundry. I did not get the Stuart privileges. Joyce had given birth to her second son, Andrew, and whenever I was at home we would have the children every Saturday morning so Joyce and her husband John could have some time together by themselves. It was fabulous for me to see my mother allow little babies to pull all her books off the shelves; little dirty fingers all over the place, food all over the kitchen walls when they were learning to feed themselves. We had never been allowed to do any of that!

By the early 1970s I had qualified as a social worker and done my first professional training at the Tavistock Clinic in London. I had a Mental Health Warrant as well as being a qualified child-care specialist. I used to visit a children's home in Kent and thought it was such a lovely drive. When my mother came to stay with me I would take her out there and when she left Liverpool she settled in Sevenoaks. Her move was a combination of things: it brought her nearer to me but I think she also wanted to get away from the memories of Liverpool. That was in 1976, and not much later the South London Art Gallery put on an exhibition of Stuart's work and Harold Wilson wrote to her about it. She was proud he took the time, for he was having a tough time in the House of Commons. But people liked her, not just for herself but for her loyalty to Stuart. And who will argue with the saying that you are returned what you give?

One day she was at Sevenoaks station waiting for her train to Charing Cross where I was to collect her when two nuns in brown habits appeared. It's rare to see Franciscan nuns and she was so amazed that she went and spoke to them. They said they had just established a mother house down the road from where she lived. She then shared with them her history and they invited her for tea the following weekend. There were two nuns there who had been in her year all that time ago in Scotland; they rooted in their cupboards and brought out photograph albums with pictures of my mother that were nearly sixty years old. From then on, life was heaven for her. I used to tease her and say to her that she had re-entered without giving up her freedom. That opened up a whole world for her, for she was a contemplative woman by nature.

My world was expanding too, and for my next training I went to America, to the Philadelphia Child Guidance Clinic. My sister and her family would visit Mother or she would go and see them in Lancashire. The rest of the time she had the nuns, and her priest. I returned from America in 1980 and found Mother very happy and settled. She would still get angry that the Beatles had hindered her efforts to promote Stuart's art, but if time had not made her less determined it had at least made her more accepting, if not understanding, about it.

And that year, she and Queenie had to be there for Aunt Mimi who had always, always loved John. Adored him and lived for him. When he was shot dead by Mark David Chapman at around 11 p.m. on 8 December 1980, as he and Yoko returned to the Dakota apartments in New York, they comforted Mimi. I was totally devasted by the news. I'm an early riser and heard it on the radio in London first thing in the morning. Drivers were keeping their headlights on as a mark of respect. John had created and cultivated a public persona that was so well defined and copiously documented that it had resisted all attempts at a rewrite. Now, with his death, it was open season. Many made him a saint, others, the revisionists of the legend, made him a dysfunctional layabout. I think that at the time of his death the latter was closer to the mark. John sat around the Dakota apartment and smoked dope, stroked his cat and himself, masturbating. I know that Cynthia and Julian were so concerned about him just before his murder that they were hoping to bring him back to Britain for some treatment. Again, what if? As with all about the Beatles, the myth of John has multiplied in the more than twenty years since his death. My mother cried with Mimi and so did I. John may have been the instrument of Stuart's death but he was also Stuart's loving friend. I could never hate or despise him. In 1980, they did indeed become blood brothers.

I still see them as young men. I think of the others that way too. It was painful to read the newspaper reports of George Harrison's battle with cancer, and the news in summer 2001 that he was not given long to live. This was not that long after nearly being killed at his own home. There is still no ordinary life for the survivors: look at George, who was so unsettled by that violent attack at his home that he put the property on the market. I can understand why: he felt invaded, his sanctuary, for all its security, violated. It's like after a burglary – your home is never quite the same place again. There has been so much misfortune around the Beatles, like Paul's wife Linda's tragic early death from cancer. I do hope his relationship with Heather Mills stays happy, for it is never easy for another person to replace a loved lost one. And conducting your relationship in the public eye is an added strain. News that they were to be married in spring 2002 was announced on television and with such a splash in the newspapers of course, adversity can be conquered. Ringo managed it with the actress Barbara Bach after the death of his former wife Maureen. And Barbara helped him overcome a dependence on alcohol. But Ringo sought help and that saved him. John never did – or, rather, never looked for conventional help.

I hate to seem morbid because that is not part of my character, but events tumble into our lives and there is not much we can do to change the more important ones. My mother died in 1983. She was seventy-six years old. It was the happiest funeral I ever went to.

She became suddenly, hugely ill with her stomach. She was asthmatic and not in the most robust of health but she wasn't diagnosed with anything. Her GP thought it was food poisoning and gave her tummy medicine but she did not improve so I went and stayed overnight with her. The next day I rang the GP and said that it looked more serious to me. An ambulance was sent, the blue flashing light and all that stuff, monitoring her blood pressure every ten minutes. She looked like she was dying. They took her down to theatre for emergency investigations. Meanwhile, I'd phoned my sister and said they'd said she didn't look like she'd live. My sister came, of course, on the train all the way from the north of England. A young doctor came to see me hours later and said,

'I'm awfully sorry to have to tell you but there's a huge growth in the bowel that must be cancer.' About half an hour later he came and said, 'I'm awfully sorry, I was looking at the wrong X-rays'. It was unbelievable.

She eventually arrived from exploratory surgery alive and with no diagnosis. They hadn't found anything. She never recovered. She went downhill and three weeks later she was dead. Never left hospital. It was in Tunbridge Wells. So for three weeks she had nil by mouth, no cigarette, and she could hardly read. She was an avid reader. She died of a pulmonary embolism. I was with her. I slept in the hospital. My sister arrived just after she died. She had been up and down for those three weeks. And the nuns and the priest. They were the same age as her, and they used to get into their Renault 5 and drive from Sevenoaks to Tunbridge Wells most days. They were just absolutely marvellous. They filled in the gaps between my sister and me. As I said, she had a happy funeral. The nuns and priest gave her a requiem Mass in Sevenoaks and then she was cremated in Tunbridge Wells. Then my sister and I gave her a reception for them all in my mother's Sevenoaks flat. There's nothing like nuns and priests to make you feel that the soul is at rest and she's out of all that pain.

Her death was very similar to that of my father. She had made her will years before she died and we had quite lively discussions with my sister because Mother wanted to be cremated, which was not common for Catholics at that time. We argued whether the Catholic Church really approved of cremation. But, oh, how she wanted to be cremated. It is such a Liverpool story. The explanation was that my brother and father were buried together in the churchyard in Huyton. There was room for one more.

But because Mother was a Catholic she couldn't be buried there. She wanted to be cremated so that we could place her ashes there with my father and my brother. My sister and I did that in the middle of a long, dark night and we still hope we're not going to be prosecuted. My brother-in-law helped. He kept an eye out.

We didn't scatter the ashes but buried the casket. We had to dig quite a decent-sized hole. And we placed Mother in the ground next to Stuart and our father. The three of them. All together again.

thirteen

Shadow of the Beatles

'Stuart will always have a special corner of my heart. A sensitive, caring young man, he was my friend and supportive ally on many occasions. His talent was outstanding and, thank God, will endure; as his memory endures with me. His life was cruelly cut short but the legacy he left behind was his work – and his enthusiasm for life, truth and love.'

Cynthia Lennon

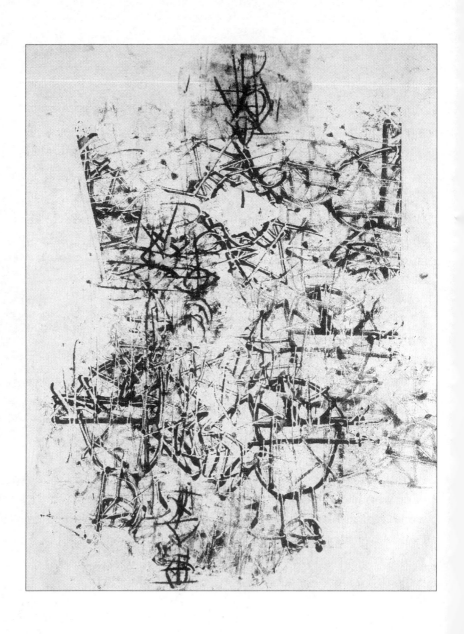

WITH MY MOTHER'S death, as sole executrix of Stuart's estate, *my* battle with the Beatles began. When the boys first became famous, my mother had warned Joyce and me: 'Don't take the Beatles on – they'll win.' She was acutely aware of the corporate power that came with so much fame.

I was now even more aware of her foreboding about dealing with the Beatles, who she felt could be a destructive force. I founded StuArt to promote Stuart's work, and my life seemed to be a series of twenty-four-hour days. I was in social work management, practising as a psychotherapist and using the time left to catalogue, organize and improve an archive that I felt would be a proper and ongoing tribute to Stuart who had died more than two decades earlier. By then the Beatles were part of all our lives. Posthumously, John had become an even greater legend. To those of us who had been around in the sixties, it was amusing to see the wonderment of another generation of pop fans, on discovering that Paul McCartney was in a group before Wings.

Nevertheless, the fascination with the Beatles and with Stuart went on: *STU – Scenes from the Life of Stuart Sutcliffe*, a play by Jeremy Stockwell and Hugh O'Neill, was presented at the Bromley Little Theatre in Kent the year my mother died. Only a few months later Mike Evans's *The Art of the Beatles* was published, and some of Stuart's work was included in an exhibition staged in Liverpool and then overseas. In 2001, Stuart's work developed a cult following in America and there was a grand display at the Govinda Gallery in Washington DC. The archive has grown but it centres on the great number of paintings and his works on paper, his drawings and sketches. Emotionally, it is the collections of letters surrounding Stuart's short life that many find most intriguing, but his art, the Hamburg period, reflects so much that was going on within him and in his outside world with Astrid and John and the Beatles.

Astrid seemed to vanish from our lives in the sixties and in a very reclusive way. After creating such lasting images of Stuart and the Beatles, she gave up photography in 1964. Later, she worked as a barmaid in Hamburg, saying she did not want to exploit her relationship with Stuart and the Beatles. She did stay in touch with John and certainly with George. In 1968, she came out of retirement and photographed George for the album of the *Wonderwall* soundtrack, which was the first recording released by Apple Records. Astrid is credited on it as Astrid Kemp – she had married Gibson Kemp, who was eight years younger and who had been involved in a rock group with Klaus Voormann. Klaus had given up technical drawing and aspired to be a rock star himself; he continued his Beatles connections for a long time. Klaus took up the bass guitar and joined up with Gibson Kemp and Paddy Chambers, who had been one of the Big Three pop group, and they performed as Paddy, Klaus and Gibson. Klaus did well and played with the Hollies and Manfred Mann. He also gave Ringo Starr guitar lessons and used his art expertise to create the album sleeve for the Beatles' *Revolver* album. There were many stories about Astrid and her lifestyle, but many may have been apocryphal. After her last visit to us in Liverpool it was thirty-two years before I was to see her again.

However, I had to deal with her legally in the mid-1980s. That was when Stuart's letters to my mother and Joyce came up for auction at Sotheby's in London. As I said, I only found out about their sale by chance. At that time, memorabilia involving Stuart were selling for substantial amounts of money at Beatles conventions and auctions. For me, money had nothing to do with these letters; they were his last letters to both my mother and Joyce. Indeed, his last letter ever was the one to Joyce. I felt it was a travesty that they would be on the auction block. I got involved in a complicated legal wrangle over them, which was my first encounter with the role and responsibilities of managing my brother's estate. It was extremely unpleasant and expensive. All the legal papers had to be translated from German, and the differences in German law were difficult and took time to deal with. It became very messy and I felt terrible. I was only trying to carry out my mother's wishes and to protect my brother's estate. In that sale, Astrid sold-off gifts that Stuart had given her and she and Klaus had also put Stuart's Hofner bass guitar – the blonde – up for sale at Sotheby's. It was bought by the Hard Rock Café, which generously loaned it to me for Stuart's 2001 exhibition in the Rock and Roll Hall of Fame. At the time of the Sotheby's auction, I agreed to let the sale go ahead providing I got my mother's letters back along with Stuart's wallet, and we would split the money from the sale of the guitar. The proceeds just about covered my legal costs. But Stuart's letters were retrieved for his estate.

Astrid did not emerge into our world again until the 1990s when the film *Backbeat* was released. It was a dramatic return. But a decade earlier the director Iain Softley had started developing that project about Stuart's life and death in Hamburg. He began by working with me not long after my mother died but then he tracked down Astrid and I feel it became more *her* film than one about Stuart and John and the Beatles. Iain Softley was the first person who managed to track her down and gain her confidence, and that was quite a scoop for him. I think that coup shifted his position on the material that was available to him. Stuart's estate had no legal standing in the development of the film, and I was devoting myself to organizing exhibitions of Stuart's art.

We staged a one-man show in 1990 in London, and Liverpool

supporters such as the author Beryl Bainbridge turned up. Around that time I contemplated doing a major book about Stuart and his life and work and, of course, his founding-member association with the Beatles. Stuart is special to me and our family and many others for his art and his life, but for millions of others it is his time with the group and his relationship with John that is of overwhelming interest. I understand that. And so did Paul, or to give him his formal title, Sir Paul McCartney. He agreed to give me an interview for the book and in doing so gave me a memory and an insight to all the sudden fame those young boys achieved. I don't know if any of them were ever taught or allowed to learn how to function, even in impolite society. When I arrived at his office in Soho Square in London it followed what seemed like an MI6 training exercise, spy manoeuvres.

I had been given exact instructions – it was like waiting for the red telephone to ring announcing a nuclear attack. I was to wait by the phone to be told when to appear at Paul's offices. The phone duly rang and I got a cab. I was shown into the reception area, up in the lift to the private offices where I waited for four hours. I was freezing and hungry. I was anxious because I had patients to see later in the day. It was before the use of mobile phones became widespread, so I had no way of easily delaying appointments; if I went off to a public telephone, he might have appeared. I asked and asked his assistants and it was always, 'it won't be long'. I saw Linda McCartney and secretaries flitting in and out. There was an artist I sort of recognized; they looked warm with all that activity. I was sitting there freezing and wondering what to do. And becoming very angry indeed. I was offered and gladly accepted a Coca-Cola. I was thinking about my great interest in talking to Paul about Stuart but also what would happen if I said that I was awfully sorry but I couldn't wait any longer, my first priority was to my patients. However, I had been made very aware that this was a privilege. I was, like my mother, trapped.

I was competing with emotions. I hadn't seen him for, oh,

centuries. At the Cavern. My first impression when I walked in was, 'Good God, isn't this beautiful? Where's the baked beans on toast and the cup of tea over the kitchen table?'

The whole of the offices of MPL Communications Ltd was beautiful with fabulous art. There might have been other, little back offices, but in terms of its order and taste and overall aesthetic it was breathtakingly gorgeous, envy-making. I was so taken with the Willem de Kooning tapestries in his inner office. Linda McCartney's father had acted in legal matters for de Kooning and that was Paul's initial connection. I don't suffer from envy but here, I have to admit, I was. These tapestries start at £3 million pounds, but I was not so in awe of the cost but in the glory of them. And that this young lad from Liverpool could own so much. But the first piece of art to startle me was a sculpture by the now Sir Eduardo Paolozzi: that was one of the big images that confronted me in Paul's office, a Paolozzi sculpture, a stainless steel torso.

When, finally, Paul came out to welcome me and scooped me up in his arms and kissed me, it disarmed me. He was wonderfully dressed, neat in something like Armani. I was still trying not to let my anger show. My first instinct was to say, 'Who the heck do you think you are to waste people's time? You can waste your own but you don't own mine.' That sort of anger, which of course I couldn't show. He disarmed me further because when I asked if I could tape-record our conversation he fixed up the tape recorder because I didn't know how to use the darned thing properly. We sat close together on a couch; there was fresh fruit on the table and he nibbled at a grape and offered me some fruit and we talked as though we were just catching up from the week before. The remarks from Paul throughout this book come from that interview.

Talking to Paul, I felt that the tension lines between him and Stuart were there from the start for Stuart intruded, in Paul's view, on himself and John; even decades on Paul was wary over how he took over the bass guitar in the Beatles and how I, my sister and, before her death, my mother viewed him and the other Beatles following Stuart's death, and also the deaths of Brian Epstein and John. When I saw him he said, 'I always felt a little strange. I don't care what everyone else thinks because I know what I know, but I do feel a little bit sorry for you and your mum.'

I think Paul leaves himself so open to criticism. In May 2001 he was reported in the newspapers as being worth more than £700 million, and you can be as useless at mathematics as me and still know that's close to a billionaire. At the same time he gave an interview to *Radio Times* complaining that Yoko Ono had, at one time, earned more from his song 'Yesterday' than he did. Paul's gripe was that he and John had signed a writing partnership contract as Lennon and McCartney when they were only twenty years old but that it was still valid and he felt he should be entitled to more from 'Yesterday', which he alone composed. He said in the BBC magazine: 'I don't feel bitter, but it's pretty terrible and wrong. They should recognize our success and alter the deal. At one point Yoko earned more from "Yesterday" than I did. It doesn't compute, especially when it is the only song that none of the Beatles had anything to do with.'

He revealed that he had asked 'as a favour' for his name to go before John's on the credits for 'Yesterday' in the hugely successful *Beatles' Anthology*.

He said Yoko refused. That didn't surprise me. None of it did. For whatever reason, there's not a lot of generosity from any of the Beatle camps. I think you have to be charitable *and* delve into the truth, to be probing *and* forgiving; you get truths from that incisiveness and generosity. Otherwise we shall never know the motives, for they pull down the blinds, put on the sunglasses, and hide what they are thinking.

Among Stuart's archive are song lyrics written in 1960 or 1961 with input from John. I suggested that Oasis, Noel and Liam Gallagher, might put music to them and release some recordings, which caused quite a disturbance in the world of the Beatles. I think the Oasis sound is the closest I've heard to the original

Beatles, and I mean that as a great compliment. Instinctively, I thought they could provide some magic by working with Stuart's lyrics, yesterday and today getting together. It seemed like a marvellous project. Yoko heard about it and immediately lawyers were brought in, trying to establish the extent of John's involvement – and rights. I don't think it is simply Yoko reacting – it is the machine. I have not pursued the idea any further. With good reason. It would have taken a mammoth legal endeavour to try to prove that these were Stuart's *original* lyrics.

It appears to me that the Beatles have always been about circling the wagons, preserving what they have. I had an extraordinary experience with them over their 1995 musical anthology which, through its sales and applauded production, proved them once again as the most marketable group ever known.

I was at a friend's house for a Friday evening dinner party when I got a surprising phone call from a lawyer representing the Beatles. The *Anthology* CD was already on sale in America and the lawyer said to me: 'We may owe you a little fee.' There was nothing about a royalty; it was a fee. And there was no mention of requiring a contract. Stuart is credited on the CD notes as part of the Beatles line-up for three of the tracks recorded at Paul's house in 1960, indicating to me that this was something special, helping it be a collectors' item as well as a fan's dream. I felt comfortable suggesting the estate should be entitled to a royalty. And you will understand that I was a little bemused when the lawyer explained there was no evidence that Stuart was on any of the tracks they had credited him with. I could not afford to bring in engineers to try to prove that a bass was present on the tracks, and I didn't even have the original material. I took legal advice but the cost of taking action against them, especially if we lost, was prohibitive: it was David against Goliath and no matter how many sling-shots we took, they had the corporate machine guns blazing back. I found myself in a no-win situation over the royalty and negotiated a settlement fee – on condition that it was not a royalty and that there was no acknowledgment whatsoever from their side that Stuart was on any of their recordings. After the legalities were over, I had to ask myself, why? Why would they behave like this? It seems so ungracious, in view of their own fame and wealth. They could have said, it's a bit hard to hear the bass on some of the recordings, but we think Stuart was on them, this was his recording as well as ours.

One newspaper said we got a settlement of £800,000. Our fee was £70,000. Part of it went to Liverpool John Moores University where we had established the Stuart Sutcliffe Fellowship Award. My mother, my sister and I have worked to establish public recognition for Stuart's work and the award was a memorial to him in the form of a scholarship for young artists, to which our friend in Chicago, Stephen Taylor, made the first donation.

I was impressed with Iain Softley's film *Backbeat*. But of course it was a film. There is perception and there is reality. Iain Softley brought Sheryl Lee who played Astrid and Stephen Dorff who was Stuart in the film to see me. The film alluded to the relationship between John and Stuart but the focus was Astrid's ménage. It is a good, arty film, but what does it say about the people? When Stephen Dorff came to see me he told me he was working with a voice coach – he had to be taught how to talk Liverpool. I said, 'Why bother?' If anything, Stuart had more of a soft Edinburgh accent. But for the movies they all had to be Scousers, didn't they? Oscar Wilde? 'Truth is rarely pure, and never simple.'

Certainly, the promotion of *Backbeat* in Japan was extravagant. The Japanese company launching and distributing the film, the Dela Corporation, also organized an exhibition of Stuart's work to coincide with the film's opening in Tokyo. There were two free-standing exhibits, one of Stuart's work and the other of Astrid's photographs. It was March 1994 when Joyce and I flew to Japan for the exhibition and the screening of the film. We had been travelling for almost a day, and were met at the airport by a chauffeur in white gloves and several young women in another car so there was a little convoy of us. They were all on walkie-talkies, radioing ahead to detail our progress into the city where we were to be met by Miyako Ejiri, the president of the distribution company. She was on the steps of the hotel as we drove up. I had met her several times in London and worked with her in getting the exhibits out to Tokyo. I liked her very much. She welcomed me warmly, kissed me on the cheek and said, 'I've got a surprise for you.'

She walked me into the hotel and there was Astrid, who I had not seen for thirty-two years. I did a double-take. It was clearly Astrid, but more than three decades separated my mental image of her and the reality of seeing Stuart's former lover as an older woman. In my mind, Astrid had never aged and it was a strange experience. She was well groomed, her hair still tightly cropped, stylishly dressed. But she was obviously nervous, which was not sur-prising. I was too. I could feel myself shaking and had goosebumps along my arms.

She was with her manager, Ulf Kruger. It was quickly established that Astrid was very anxious about doing interviews for the Press – we all had personal translators – and I would need to take on most of that because Astrid was vulnerable and delicate. She was lovely to Joyce. I was handled with a bit of suspiciousness, I think. I am a bit too like my mother. We suggested dinner but they countered with a drink, which we thought was a bit of a push-off until it became clear, when we saw the astronomical food prices, that they were just trying to be considerate. Ulf moved himself away from the table and sort of hung around in the background. Then Astrid, later, let it all come out – like a projectile vomit.

She said my mother had called her a high-class whore. That didn't surprise me – I knew my mother had said that to her. I was present. Astrid repeated it again and again and we just let her go on. Essentially, it was about how my mother had said she had led Stuart astray and into this arty, farty, existentialist stuff. She said my mother had accused her of having an affair with George. She didn't say she had or she hadn't but her tone implied that she thought it was an outrageous suggestion. When she stopped, Joyce and I pointed out to her that she seemed to have forgotten that we loved our mother and we found her attack very upsetting and worrying because she clearly had not resolved it in any way after all these years. I said it was not good for her to be hanging on to such ferocious anger with a person who was dead. At that point she told me she had begun to see a therapist and I thought, 'Good, about time.'

I did tell her I understood my mother's feelings, although I never encouraged her in those thoughts because I didn't want her to be more upset than she was. My mother's feeling was that Stuart had thrown his life away for the Beatles and for a woman who it *appeared to her* had moved on too quickly. Perhaps this was unfair; Astrid published a book in 2000 and in it she talked once again of Stuart as the love of her life. But in my opinion Astrid showed insensitivity over the delayed return of Stuart's property and his last letters to my mother, which all began to come together for me when I walked into Stuart's exhibition in Tokyo.

The first thing that confronted me was a large photograph by Astrid of Gibson Kemp. Gibson Kemp? He was the main photographic image as you walked into the room. It didn't make any sense. This was a Stuart exhibition, to complement the *Backbeat* film. There was also a big photograph of Astrid and George on prominent display. And one of her and Jackie Lomax from the Undertakers dated from October 1962, six months after Stuart died. Miyako Ejiri walked around the room and told Astrid to place the pictures in more discreet locations. And put Stuart centre stage, as it were. It was a most bizarre engagement and certainly in no way as joyous as when Stuart and John were reunited in the twenty-first century at the Rock and Roll Hall of Fame and Museum in Cleveland, Ohio.

postscript

Together Again

'Stuart is a vital part of the answer to why and how
earth-shattering things happened with the Beatles.'

Shelagh Johnston, general manager, 'The Beatles Story', 2001

YES, THERE HAVE been heartaches over the years because of Stuart's vital role in the story of the Beatles, but I could never deny the good side that resulted through people I have encountered, many of whom are now great friends. Often, like the best parties, it was never pre-planned. The wonderful feature writer Maureen Cleave I met for professional reasons. She was working on an article about psychotherapy and was told I could help.

Maureen wrote the first ever London story about the Beatles, 'Why the Beatles create all that frenzy' was the headline, which appeared in the London *Evening Standard*, on 2 February 1963. Later, she conducted the famous John Lennon interview in which John said 'We're more popular than Jesus now,' which was published in the *Standard* on 4 March 1966. At first, she had no idea of my Beatles connection. We met at the Halcyon Hotel in Holland Park, London, for coffee and to talk about psychotherapy. We made small talk and, on the second cup of coffee, she said, 'You're Stu Sutcliffe's sister.' We did the professional stuff and then talked about Stuart and the other Beatles. She was so enjoyable. At the time, in 1996, I was publishing a coffee-table art book about Stuart, and darling Michael Kenny had arranged for there to be a launch party at the Royal Academy of Art. I invited Maureen.

She turned up with a brown-paper carrier bag and from it she produced a battered Elvis LP. It was 'Heartbreak Hotel' from 1956.

On the front was the name Stuart Sutcliffe, scribbled by Stuart. He had lent his LP to John Lennon who had given it to Maureen in the sixties. More than thirty years later she had looked it out and thought it should be returned to Stuart. It is now in the Rock and Roll Hall of Fame and museum.

As is almost everything of Stuart's, other than the most treasured family things that Joyce and I wish to keep. Getting all of it in one place at the same time took some achievement. I had allowed an art dealer in Washington to have some of Stuart's work for display. Other pieces were in Liverpool, the location of the long-running 'The Beatles Story' exhibition. And that is where Terry Sampson and Shelagh Johnston, come into Stuart's story.

Shelagh is the general manager of the 'The Beatles Story' and Terry is a director of the ongoing exhibition that is one of the most visited attractions in Liverpool. They are always on alert for new material that will add to the telling of the story of the Beatles, especially archive items with a direct connection. Terry had read in the *Mail on Sunday* that an exhibition of Cynthia's drawings was being held in March 1999 at the KDK Gallery in Portobello Road, London, and was curious. I had an interest in the gallery and helped out there, but when Terry called on the Monday we were closed – always closed on a Monday: it must be my hairdressing background. Terry was surprised, because Cynthia's show had got a lot of publicity the day before. Thankfully, he was persistent. He decided to visit the gallery on the Tuesday and that's when I met him.

On one wall were Cynthia's drawings and on the other the work of her close friend, from Liverpool Art School, Phyllis Mackenzie. Terry says he was immediately interested although many of the works had red dots on them, indicating that they were sold. Terry told me he was from 'The Beatles Story' and I told him I knew Shelagh. He got out his mobile phone and called Shelagh. They agreed she should come to the gallery as soon as possible – the number of Cynthia's drawings without red dots was dwindling. Shelagh arrived from Liverpool the next morning and thought that

Cynthia's work represented a lovely account of the early life of the Beatles. She said they were as close to the Beatles' inner circle as you could get, full of detail and emotion. They bought eight drawings, all that were available, for 'The Beatles Story' and made a special section at the exhibition for them. Cynthia attended that August bank holiday weekend opening in 1999 – by pure chance coinciding with a Beatles convention in the city. It was a huge success.

By now I had grown fond of Terry and Shelagh and had earlier shown them Stuart's work, which was in another area of the gallery. Shelagh was intrigued by Stuart's material from Liverpool, everything from the training books and the drawings to the canvases. It showed, she said, his development at close range. She said she knew a lot about Stuart but told me:

It was when I saw his things and the letters to you and Joyce and his mother I knew it was a treasure chest of the origins of the Beatles. One thing that Terry and I always try to focus on in 'The Beatles Story' is that we are telling the story of the Beatles – not George Harrison with his gardening expeditions or Ringo and Thomas the Tank Engine. What they do now is fairly much diluted for the worldwide audience visiting Liverpool. They don't want that. They want to see the Beatles and touch them and get as close to, discover, what the Beatles were and how special their music is.

The Beatles are history: they started and they ended. We tell the story from their births, their family backgrounds, how they met each other, all in the utmost detail up until 1969 and 1970 and the break-up. As individuals it is almost a weekly update. But the people who come to Liverpool are making that journey for the Beatles until 1970 and that must be our focus. The Stuart collection is as close to the embryonic Beatles as you can get and helps people find out why they were so different from all the other groups and what made them different. It is an essential part of the Beatles' story. I do believe that Stuart was of immense influence, highly inspirational; his own artistic style and design and fashion-consciousness was terribly strong and affected them all, especially John Lennon.

And as John was probably the strongest mind in the band at that time I think he took up the challenge that Stuart's inspiration and ideas presented to them. John was the conduit of Stuart's influence to the others. John trusted Stuart and his opinions and that's where John got his security from. Stuart would not bullshit him. Stuart is a vital part of the answer to why and how things happened with the Beatles. I believe that, and other people do because it makes sense of the whole phenomenon. It wasn't we're-so-lucky-we're-all-here-on-the-same-day-and-it's-worked. There's a little bit of fate that Brian Epstein walked in when he did, but he had to hear what he heard. He could have walked straight out again.

I was delighted with everything Shelagh said, as it echoed my own feelings. Terry also pointed out how curious it was that he had walked into the KDK Gallery, like Brian going to the Cavern. Intrigue and fate mixed together. Terry did not get grumpy that we were closed, he made an effort. He told me that it was an *instinct*.

We met again two weeks later and they asked me – with a trepidation they only admitted later – if I would ever consider allowing them to display the Stuart collection as part of 'The Beatles Story'. I was thrilled. They created an area for Stuart and his work and memorabilia, knocking down walls and taking up precious storage space to ensure it was given a marvellous display. In February 1999, 'The Beatles Story' – that is, Shelagh and Terry – had managed after three and a half years of negotiations with a private collector to borrow John's upright Steinway piano on which he composed 'Imagine'. They created an exhibit in which Stuart and John's early lives were mingled and told the story of the art school days and Hamburg and ended with the 'Imagine' piano. In between, book-ended by Stuart and John, was the Beatles' story. They had decided to dedicate the display, Shelagh said, to the two Beatles who were no longer with us. She told me, 'They stood together very comfortably. The media liked it, the public like it, we liked it.'

I liked it for Stuart. I felt he got the recognition he deserved – and in his own backyard, which is usually the hardest place to achieve your due. I thought it was a working-through of all that had happened with Stuart, there was a completion of the circle. But more was to happen through Terry and Shelagh.

The private collector who owned the 'Imagine' piano sold it, at auction, to George Michael in October 2000 for £1.45 million pounds. It was the highest price any piece of Beatle memorabilia has ever been sold for. When it left 'The Beatles Story' the journey of Stuart's collection to the Rock and Roll Hall of Fame began. It was Terry's coup. In 1995 he had read in their business plan that the Rock and Roll Hall of Fame intended to mount a travelling exhibition that people around the world could borrow. Terry went to Cleveland and told the directors there of the extreme interest of 'The Beatles Story' in any complementary travelling exhibit. Time went slowly but finally Jim Henke, the chief curator of the Rock and Roll Hall of Fame, flew over to Liverpool. I met him along with Terry and Shelagh. Terry told me, 'Jim Henke was absolutely knocked out by the Stuart collection. In three days we showed him all the sites – from Penny Lane to Strawberry Fields and beyond. On his last night in Liverpool we had a long dinner and he told me that my dream could come true. We could exchange the Sutcliffe collection for something from Cleveland.'

Sometime, Stuart was going to join John in America – but it happened faster than any of us imagined. I think Jim Henke spotted, as Terry and Shelagh had, that the Stuart collection was cornerstone stuff in the early history of the Beatles that people did not know about. But I had to tell all of them that the collection was not complete; it had never all been together in one place. There were many items, that had been on display for the *Backbeat* promotion in Tokyo in 1994, still in America: 40 per cent of the total collection was in Washington DC where I had left it, awaiting plans for exhibitions to be mounted. It was all art work, for I had kept to my mother's wishes that Stuart's art and his memorabilia would not be displayed together until fifteen years after her death. Remember, she wanted his art to have its chance without the Beatles.

I agreed for Terry and Shelagh to go and see the material available in Washington and to facilitate, if they could, bringing all the collection together for 'The Beatles Story' in Liverpool. Some of the collection was in storage in Maryland and the rest in a gallery in Washington DC. There were complications but Terry and Shelagh said they would go and arrange it all themselves. My professional mentor Marianne Walters, who I met in 1977 when she was a visiting consultant at the Tavistock Clinic and who had taught me in Philadelphia had returned to Washington. The three of them linked up and arranged trucks and drivers to pull the collection together. It sounds trite written like that, but it was a mammoth job going through inventories and checking and packing the paintings and other works. Against all the odds they pulled it off and retrieved parts of the collection that I was so concerned about. It was all together and safe.

After their great success there was disappointment, but only short-lived. The space available in Liverpool for the exhibition had been lost. But suddenly the Rock and Roll Hall of Fame had an opportunity to stage it in May 2001, and instantly Terry and Shelagh decided to accept that chance.

The Hall of Fame could only accommodate 80 per cent of the collection but did a magnificent job. I had made a pledge to myself to auction it and, seeing it so perfectly showcased in Cleveland, I knew that it was a good decision. Soon, finally, I would be able to remember Stuart as my brother rather than someone I had to protect, as a piece of Beatles' property. There was no great release, no road to Damascus moment, but I felt easier with myself. Perhaps the burden was lifting. And the collection, this part of Stuart would be separate from me but I felt, should have a permanent home; the interest in the Beatles is as phenomenal as they were. I arranged for Fleetwood Owen – Mick Fleetwood of Fleetwood Mac and sales expert Ted Owen – to take charge of the sale, which was the first collection of any individual member of the Beatles to be sold.

So, as you would imagine, my mind was packed with thoughts and memories as I drove down Highway 71 through the sky-scrapers of Cleveland on a sunny evening and arrived at the Rock and Roll Hall of Fame and Museum on 14 May 2001. I had been there before to help set up the exhibits but had always used a side entrance. For this big night I was escorted to the front door and into the Hall. It all looked so different. There were crowds of fans and dignitaries from the city. People had flown in from all over America. When they begin an exhibition they do it with grand style.

Up ahead of me was a forty-foot-high poster of Stuart. Hanging above him was a giant poster of John. The big photograph of John is the fun one where he has a marigold in one eye. That, I thought, was appropriate. John and Paul both have paintings in the Royal Academy and the Tate but Stuart does not. I felt that maybe John somewhere was saying to Stuart, 'Forget the Royal Academy – welcome to the Rock and Roll Hall of Fame.' Which, given their story, would have provoked one of John's great big grins. A mari-gold moment. They certainly were together again in Cleveland.

John had always said that he looked up to Stuart because Stuart always told him the truth. Now, glancing up in the giant entrance of the Hall, Stuart was looking up at John. Perhaps that was right.

Bibliography

Best, Pete, and Doncaster, Patrick: *Beatle! The Pete Best Story* (New York, Dell, 1985).

Brown, Peter, and Gaines, Steven: *The Love You Make* (London, Macmillan, 1983).

Brown, Tony: *Jimi Hendrix: A Visual Documentary* (London, Omnibus, 1992).

Bugliosi, Vincent: *Helter Skelter: The Manson Murders* (Harmondsworth, Penguin, 1977).

Clarke, Donald: *The Penguin Encyclopedia of Popular Music* (London, Viking, 1989).

Cohn, Nik: *A WopBopaLooBop AlopBamBoom: Pop from the Beginning* (London, Paladin, 1970).

Coleman, Ray: *Brian Epstein, the Man who Made the Beatles* (London, Viking, 1989).

Coleman, Ray: *John Lennon* (London, Futura, 1985).

Davies, Hunter: *The Beatles: The Authorised Biography* (London, Heinemann, 1968; reissue Arrow Paperback, 1997).

Faithfull, Marianne: *Faithfull* (London, Michael Joseph, 1994).

Fawcett, Anthony: *John Lennon, One Day at a Time* (New York, Grove, 1976).

Fleetwood, Mick, with Davis, Stephen: *Fleetwood: My Adventures with Fleetwood Mac* (London, Sidgwick and Jackson, 1990).

Frame, Pete: *The Beatles and Some Other Guys: Rock Family Trees of the Early Sixties* (London, Omnibus Press, 1997).

Furlong, June, and Block, Jill: *June, A Life Story* (London, APML, 2000).

Garfield, Simon: *Expensive Habits, The Dark Side of the Music Industry* (London, Faber & Faber, 1986).

Giuliano, Geoffrey: *Dark Horse* (London, Bloomsbury, 1989).

Giuliano, Geoffrey: *Blackbird, The Life and Times of Paul McCartney* (New York, Dutton, 1991).

Giuliano, Geoffrey: *Lennon in America* (London, Robson Books, 2000).

Goldman, Albert: *The Lives of John Lennon* (London, Bantam, 1988).

Harrison, George: *I Me Mine* (New York, Simon & Schuster, 1980).

Ironside, Virginia: *Chelsea Bird* (London, Secker & Warburg, 1964).

Leigh, Spencer: *Let's Go Down to the Cavern: The Story of Liverpool's Merseybeat* (Liverpool, Bluecoat Press, 1988).

Lennon, Cynthia: *A Twist of Lennon* (London, Star, 1978).

Lewisohn, Mark: *The Complete Beatles Chronicle*, (London, Pyramid Books, 1992).

Macdonald, Ian: *Revolution in the Head: The Beatles' Records and the Sixties* (London, Fourth Estate, 1994).

Martin, George: *All You Need Is Ears* (London, Macmillan, 1979).

Masters, Brian: *The Swinging Sixties* (London, Constable, 1985).

Miles, Barry: *Paul McCartney, Many Years From Now* (London, Secker & Warburg, 1997).

Napier-Bell, Simon: *You Don't Have to Say You Love Me* (London, New English Library, 1982).

Norman, Philip: *Shout!* (London, Elm Tree, 1981).

Norman, Philip: *Elton* (London, Hutchinson, 1991).

Pang, May, and Edwards, Henry: *Loving John, The Untold Story* (London, Warner, 1983).

Quant, Mary: *Quant by Quant* (London, Cassell, 1966).

Sheff, David: *Last Interview* (London, Sidgwick & Jackson, 2000).

Shevy, Sandra: *The Other Side of Lennon* (London, Sidgwick and Jackson, 1990).

Spencer, Terence: *It Was Thirty Years Ago Today* (London, Bloomsbury, 1994).

Taylor, Alistair: *Yesterday: the Beatles Remembered* (London, Sidgwick and Jackson, 1988).

Thompson, Douglas: *Cilla Black: Bobby's Girl* (London, Simon and Schuster, 1998).

Thompson, Phil: *The Best of Cellars. The Story of the World Famous Cavern Club* (Liverpool, Bluecoat, 1994).

Tynan, Kathleen: *The Life of Kenneth Tynan* (London, Weidenfeld & Nicolson, 1987).

Vollmer, Jurgen: *From Hamburg to Hollywood* (Guildford, Genesis Publications, 1997).

Williams, Allan: *The Man Who Gave the Beatles Away* (London, Coronet, 1976).

Index